moon
city
Review

2023

Year of the Black Rabbit by Shen Chen Hsieh
Pencil drawing and digital paint, 6 inches by 9 inches. 2023.

Moon City Review
2023

Moon City Review is a publication of Moon City Press, sponsored by the Department of English at Missouri State University, and is distributed by the University of Arkansas Press. Exchange subscriptions with literary magazines are encouraged. The editors of *Moon City Review* contract First North American Serial Rights, all rights reverting to the writers upon publication. The views expressed by authors in *Moon City Review* do not necessarily reflect the opinions of its editors, Moon City Press, or the Department of English at Missouri State University.

Submissions are considered at https://mooncitypress.submittable.com/ submit. For more information, please consult www.moon-city-press. com.

Cover designed by Shen Chen Hsieh.
Text copyedited by Karen Craigo.

moon city press
Department of English
Missouri State University

Staff

Editor
Michael Czyzniejewski

Fiction Editor
Joel Coltharp

Flash Fiction Editor
Michael Czyzniejewski

Graphic Narrative Editor
Jennifer Murvin

Nonfiction Editor
John Turner

Assistant Nonfiction Editor
Jennifer Murvin

Poetry Editor
Sara Burge

Assistant Editors

Daniel Abramovitz
Hannah Baker
Taylor Barnhart
Steve Booker
Shane Brooks
Nicole Brunette
Molly Del Rossi
Anna Edwards
Alexander Elleman
Julia Feuerborn
Jessica Flanigan

Amy Gault
Rebecca Harris
James Heil
Abigail Jensen
Mikaela Koehler
William LaPage
Jueun Lee
Sarah Lewis
Alyssa Malloy
Rachel McClay

Sidney Miles
Sarah Padfield
Hailey Pedersen
Erin Pierce
Mar Prax
Eli Slover
Shannon Small
Meg Spring
Cam Steilen
Emma Jane Sullivan
Sean Turlington

Student Editors

Giovanni Acosta
Emma Bishop
David Brockway
Jeremy Burnett
Rachel Lacey
Olivia Fowler

Holly Jones
Harrison Kayne
Savannah Keller
Alexia Laramore
Makayla Malachowski
Blake Peery
Kayla Purdome

Kylie Purdome
Danielle Ragsdale
Clay Thornton
Sierra Voiles
Siciley Wilson
Georgia Grace Wright

Advisory Editors

James Baumlin   W.D. Blackmon   Lanette Cadle   Marcus Cafagña   Alan Tinkler

Table of Contents

Janelle Drumwright

Terra Incognita

The day the first boat appeared on the horizon, we didn't know what to make of it. It was small and white and empty like the seashells that dotted our shores. But it did not seem adrift. Rather, it cut through the waves with a sense of purpose. Slowly, one by one, we broke from our chores, thatching the roofs of our huts, gathering still-green coconuts, chopping firewood for evening, and stood side by side along the shore, a murmur of excitement threading through our mouths.

Several hours passed before the boat came close enough to haul in. By then the blood-orange sun had sunk below the horizon, and our night fires were roaring along the beach, light and shadow dancing across our faces. If anyone had been riding in that boat, the blazes might have looked like a welcome, but they were also a warning. We were soft but also hard, like the abalones we scooped from the sea. A few of the stronger swimmers among us ran out into the waves, met the boat, and hauled it to shore.

We swarmed the boat like ants and ran our hands along its rough-hewn wood, our fingers lingering in the divots and dings from a journey we could not fathom. The bleached white vessel was long and narrow, a length of twenty steps when we placed heel to toe. Because of the darkness, it was with our hands, not our eyes, that we discovered the carving in the seat.

Bring a torch!

As we swept the flame over the seat's surface, the intricately cut letters with curling ends emerged from the darkness:

Galena

A hush fell over us as we all turned to face her. Galena was quiet, smart, trustworthy. We liked sitting next to her on hot days, with her fanning palm fronds toward our faces so we could feel the air move across our cheeks while we mended fishing nets. At night, when our work was done, she would polish broken coral and string the pieces into necklaces and bracelets. We touched the cool, smooth beads that gripped our throats and wrists.

Galena stepped forward, the light of the torch igniting a spark in the dark pools of her eyes and glinting off her hair. She clasped the bow in her hands like a greeting, then circled it slowly, taking in all the angles and textures, as if trying to coax the secrets from the wood. *Where have you come from? Who sent you? Why me?*

As we watched, we could not help measuring ourselves against her. We did not know why she had been chosen to receive this mysterious gift, but it made us feel like we were lacking. Galena was not the most talented among us. She was not the strongest swimmer, nor the most skilled hunter, nor an expert cook. While she was good at many things, there was nothing about her that seemed to make her worthy of something the rest of us, her friends, her sisters, were not.

Someone broke the silence with a clap of celebration, and we quickly joined in. After all, we could be happy for Galena while still feeling sorry for ourselves. Perhaps, even at that very moment, our own worthiness was being judged by our reactions to her good fortune by something larger than ourselves. To be jealous would make us less deserving than we already felt.

Galena, get in!

It's been made just for you!

Isn't it beautiful?

The boat was shifting restlessly in the shallows, so we extended our hands to help her climb in and held her steady until she found her balance. She gazed at us with the newfound benevolence of knowing she was favored, in a way the rest of us were not. But as she took her seat, the sea suddenly surged forward, then rapidly retreated, sucking the sand from beneath our feet and knocking us into the water, the powerful current dragging the boat back out to sea. As she was swept from the shore, the boat moved once again with purpose, but at a much greater speed than which it had arrived. We cried out her name, tossing our words to her like a rope.

Wait! She scrambled to the back of the boat, the fire flashing in her eyes. *Where is it taking me? I'm not ready! I haven't said goodbye!*

We wanted to race after her, to pull her back, to keep her with us, but we were no match for the boat's speed and momentum as it carried her towards her new destiny. *Hurry,* we urged one another, and started gathering whatever supplies were in reach—coconuts, a hollowed-out gourd for water, a sleeping mat—and piled them into a fishing net. We did not know where the boat was taking Galena, but we could not send her empty-handed. We quickly handed the net to Rubie, our fastest, strongest swimmer, and she raced into the sea, legs pumping as fast as she could go, the supplies bouncing against her back.

The clouds overhead parted to reveal a small pearl of moon, which cast a corridor of light along the water, leading toward the horizon. Galena was a ways out now, her calls to us muffled by the crashing of the surf, her words carried away on the back of the breeze. If Rubie didn't hurry, it would be too late to reach her. Rubie's arms cut through the waves like shark fins, zipping her forward with each pull, gaining distance on the boat.

We stood on the beach, eyes transfixed on the two figures in the water, some of us covering our mouths, others clasping each other's hands or waists. When Rubie finally reached Galena and swung the net into the boat, we all cheered. *We love you, Galena! Be brave!* We watched as Galena grasped for Rubie's hand, as though Rubie might tow her back to shore, but Rubie was already fatigued from her swim, and still had to make it back. Their hands squeezed briefly before Rubie let go, pushing off from the boat and heading back to shore. Clouds passed over the moon once more, and Galena and her boat were absorbed into the darkness.

It was impossible to sleep that night. Gusts swirled through our village, kicking up sand, rustling fronds, tickling our hair across our faces. We alternated between worrying about Galena, what creatures or storms or tests might lay before her, and fantasizing about where she might be headed. No one had ever left our little island before; we didn't need to. It had everything we needed—food, shelter, sun, water, each other. *But what else was out there? Was there more? What were we missing?*

Over the following days, the fourteen of us left behind felt Galena's absence acutely, but perhaps no one more than Kyli, who had shared a hut with Galena. That first night, unable to face their empty hut alone, Kyli had slept in the adjacent hut, where we made room for her on our grass mats. The warmth and pressure of our backs against her own, our light snoring and steady breathing, helped her feel less alone. She continued to sleep there every night after that, none of us complaining about the cramped quarters because the extra body helped to fill the void left in all of us.

Galena's hut became a makeshift shrine. Each morning, we left offerings of fresh-cut mango, sea-salt polished stones, shells with intricate patterns, flowers bursting with color. We left them in hopes that whatever had taken Galena from us would keep her from harm, that she would be blessed, that she would be happy. But we would be lying if we did not admit that it was also for ourselves. For the first time in our lives, we were considering our own worthiness, and to be, or at least appear, kind and selfless seemed like it might curry favor with whatever it was that held up the stars and the moon in the night sky.

As time passed, we stopped thinking about Galena or imagining where she was as often and instead began to imagine boats of our own with our names carved into the seats. We wanted to be chosen the way she had. Some of us imagined giant rafts with brilliant white billowing sails, while others pictured sleek, black boats jetting through the water at speeds that would rival the dolphins, and still others dreamed of rowboats festooned with flowers, shells, and shining pebbles to welcome us aboard.

The air grew warm and thick with moisture. The mangoes ripened on the trees. The temperament of the sea swung from volatile to placid and back again. Our hair grew a hand length longer, our skin two shades deeper, and the calluses on our palms thickened. The memory and excitement of the boat faded like Galena had into the horizon.

It was early dawn, just a sliver of sun glinting off the ocean like a blade, when yelling and banging on the walls of our huts roused us from our slumber. It was Lynet, who was often up an hour or two before the rest of us to take long swims in near silence, causing the commotion. *Get up! Get up! There's another boat!*

It felt as though she had doused us with cold water, and we scrambled to our feet, some of us knocking our heads on the roofs of our huts, others of us tripping over each other in our rush to the beach, our eyes not fully open yet.

At the water's clear edge sat a bright blue rowboat with thin yellow striping along its sides. A large wooden oar stretched on either side, staked into the sand as if in defiance of the outgoing tide.

Is there a name?

Who is it for?

It's mine—I just know it!

Lynet, who'd had a head start, made it to the boat first, and clambered aboard to check the seat for a carving. No sooner had she gotten both feet in the hull then the boat abruptly tipped to the side and dumped her onto the wet sand, a shriek of surprise escaping her mouth.

In those fleeting few seconds that it took Lynet to clamber back to her feet, each of our names still hung in the air as a shimmering possibility. It was the golden moment in which we all knew there was a boat, and that it was beautiful, and that it could be for any of us. We also knew it was the moment of weightlessness before the plummet. In our hearts, we did not really want the singular certainty of a name, but rather, to linger where it was all of our names and none of our names carved there in the smooth, polished wood.

But soon enough, Lynet was leaning into the boat, which had righted itself after dumping her out, as though tugged by invisible rope.

It's for … Addy!

And just like that, our fragile bubbles of hope popped, and our hearts sunk to our stomachs, heavy as stones. Addy, who was short and stocky with freckles scattered across her shoulders and the bridge of her nose, emitted a sound somewhere between a gasp of shock and a cry of victory. We raised the pitch of our voices to cover our disappointment as we gathered around her to offer our congratulations. But we wore smiles that felt more like grimaces, and we feared they looked that way, too.

Addy started embracing those of us closest to her. We told ourselves that the reason we felt like we couldn't breathe was because she was holding us so tightly. Then she threw herself across the bow, her cheek pressed flat against the salt-strewn wood with her eyes closed in rapture, as though she were reuniting with a loved one she had not seen for a long time.

Stop! Lynet cried, and we heard the raw edge in her voice, the agitation masked as warning. She cleared her throat, then added brightly, *First, we must give you a proper send-off!*

Our best hunters returned that afternoon with a boar, which we roasted on a spit over the fire until the fat dripped with a hiss into the flames and the meat began to fall from the bone. We lounged in a circle in the cool shade of the banyan trees, our limbs draped over one another like a basket weave as we feasted on the ripe bounty we had gathered—mangoes, cherimoyas, sapodillas, the fruit juice dripping down our chins. We drank endless cups of the soursop drink we made for special occasions and wove Addy's straw-colored hair into elaborate braids that wrapped her head like a crown, accented with small red flowers that we tucked into the miniature nests where the strands met.

As the sun began its descent, we built a bonfire so tall the flames could almost lick the tops of the nearby palms. Addy sat perched atop a makeshift throne of banyan branches and large rocks, a wreath of white blossoms forming a halo around her head. Her eyes sparkled in the firelight, and she laughed loudly and unapologetically at old stories and new jokes, her head tilted back as far as it would go. She was like a spirit visiting us from another realm, taking our shape for one last evening before she evaporated into mist.

As the moon climbed higher in the sky, one by one, we offered her our gifts—a pouch of herbs to treat ailments, a dolphin carved from driftwood, a bouquet of her favorite flowers.

One by one, we offered her our blessings—to be safe, to be healthy, to be happy, to be loved, to be at peace.

One by one, we kissed her on the forehead, the palm, the cheek, and embraced her for what we assumed would be the last time— knowledge that held both power and pain, as we thought of Galena disappearing into the night with nothing more than a quick squeeze from Rubie's hand.

When the bonfire had burned down to just a pile of glowing embers and we caught ourselves yawning behind our hands and over our shoulders, we knew it was time. We gathered our gifts, linked arms with those nearest us, and slowly made our way down to the water, Addy at the center of our chain, the rest of us flaring out behind her like birds in formation. One of us began to sing, and with every step we took, more voices joined her:

Oh sister, may the sun shine bright for all your days to come
And when you hear the breeze through leaves recognize our hum
Oh sister, may the sea stay calm for all your eves to come
And when you hear the waves at night recognize our drum

We filled the boat with our offerings and hugged her one last time, her crown of flowers snagging in our hair. *We love you*, we whispered with wet eyes and trembling chins. *Safe passage. Good luck. Don't forget us.*

Addy pressed her hand to her throat, as though trying to dislodge something stuck there, but all that escaped was a whimper. Wiping her tears away, she gingerly stepped into the boat, careful not to crush any of the gifts at her feet. When she took her seat, the oars sprang to life and pushed the boat off the sand into the sea, carrying her toward the star-studded horizon with long, steady pulls. *I love you all*, she called between sobs, then pressed her hands to her mouth before extending them out to us. We waved until the silhouette of the boat was swallowed by the darkness of deeper waters. We wondered if she was still staring back at us, or if she had already turned to face the endless horizon.

As we trudged to our huts, we felt like scraped-out gourds, emptied of everything except the few scattered seeds of jealousy that had first taken root when Galena left. And we were exhausted by the fanfare, by the ongoing battle between how we felt on the inside and how we were supposed to look on the outside. That night we were too tired, too heartsick, to even dream.

More boats came. Sometimes they were only a fortnight apart; other times whole seasons passed. We didn't know where the boats came from, nor where they went. All we knew was that they arrived on our shores and carried away our sisters, one by one, the name of the next chosen one carved in the seat. Sometimes the vessels appeared at daybreak, a hole punched in the horizon. Other times they slipped ashore in the cover of night, noiseless amidst the lapping of the waves.

For those of us left, the arrival of the boats was a seemingly endless disappointment. As our numbers dwindled and our patience and enthusiasm waned, the sendoffs grew shorter and less grandiose. Those who found their names carved into the seats began to feel relief more than anything else. They would no longer have to wait, to bide their time, to wonder *Why not me?* They would finally be able to move on to whatever awaited them. The island began to feel less like our home and more like a holding pen.

Do they ever think of us? we wondered. *Do they pity us? Are they all reunited somewhere, enjoying each other's company?*

We learned some hard lessons, too. During Liann's goodbye celebration, Rhea snuck away to try to steal her boat. We do not know all the details of what happened—only the single set of footprints leading down to the beach, and Liann's boat capsized just past the break line. The boat eventually righted itself and returned to shore, but we never saw Rhea again.

When Eula's boat arrived, instead of being excited, she was terrified and refused to board it. We tried to show her compassion, to soothe her, but inside we were livid. How could she refuse the very thing that all of us spent our days and nights yearning for, dreaming about?

The next day, a violent storm rolled in and thrashed our island with high winds, thunder, and lightning, ripping our camp apart without abatement. We lost our huts, our food stores, our tools. We'd never seen anything like it. Sudden gusts ripped out the banyan trees by their roots, sent giant boulders rolling down the green hills. The rain lashed our faces, our bare arms, our calves. We knew we would not survive much longer unless the storm let up. On the third consecutive night, cold and tired and hungry and angry, we seized Eula, tied her up, and carried her kicking and screaming to the boat. There were no feast, no offerings, no singing.

Please, she cried. *I don't want to! I can't!*

We tossed her into the boat and pushed it into the churning waves, her screams overpowered by crashes of thunder.

By the next morning, the sky had cleared, the sun had come out, and the swollen earth around us began to empty.

Instead of living, we waited. To pass the time, we tried to figure out some rhyme or reason to it all—why the boats arrived when they did, why some of us were picked and others were left waiting, what made one person worthier than another. But we could not find any rules or patterns, whether in talents or looks, body type or skills, demeanor or virtues. But we could not shake the feeling that we must have failed in some way or lacked something that would make us deserving of what the others had received. So we tried to change ourselves in the hopes that the next boat would be for us.

Some of us ate less to become thin, like Cheyene (Boat 3), while others ate more to grow stronger, like Rubie (Boat 7).

Some of us retreated to the shade, so that we might lighten, like Liann (Boat 10), but others darkened in the sun to match Esme's shade of bronze (Boat 8).

Some of us gave up meat, like Dayal (Boat 13), while others refused to eat anything else, like Eula (Boat 5).

We tried to make coral necklaces like Galena.

We took early morning swims like Lynet (12).

We learned to throw a spear like Mendha (4).

Each time a new boat arrived, none of us could say with certainty whether what the chosen one had done had worked or if the timing were merely what it had always been destined to be, but these activities gave us a sense of control, even if it was a false sense, and helped us pass the time.

And then one day, there were just two of us left: Ambra and me.

In the early days, before our sisters began to disappear, Ambra and I had not been as close as we had with the others. But as our numbers shrank, and those of us left spent more and more time together, our disappointment, our sadness, and our insecurities drew us closer to one another, tightened our circle like a knot. Ambra and I developed an easy silence with one another. We understood the rocky terrain of the other's jagged heart and desolate mind because our inner landscapes were the same. We knew what a stifled whimper in the darkest part of the night meant. We felt the same fledgling hope each time we glanced at the horizon, and the same crushing disappointment when we saw nothing there. We both carried the burden of time on our backs as the sun and moon chased each other across the heavens, never to be caught.

It was our only comfort, really, having someone else in the same situation—it made being left behind feel less like a personal slight and more like simple misfortune. We didn't talk about it much, but sometimes, at night, before we closed our eyes to sleep, we would utter the things we couldn't say in daylight. Within the walls of our hut, the world shrank to the size of a clamshell, and that world felt safe.

How long has it been since the last boat? Ambra asked one night, hands clasped behind her head, staring up at the roof, dark, frizzy curls fanning her face.

I remember dragon fruit in Tarrah's boat, I said. *So at least four seasons.*

It was not the longest time that had passed between boats, but it was close, and we both knew it.

We're probably due for a boat soon, then, don't you think? I asked.

Ambra sighed, then pressed her palms to her eyes. *I can't say,* she said.

Why? I asked.

To be certain of anything would seem an invitation to ruin it.

Two more seasons passed, and I began to scan the horizon less and less. Getting my hopes up was a painful lesson I'd been learning over and over again for many seasons now, and I was too raw, too tired to keep doing it. It was a blister that would only get worse unless I stopped chafing it. I was coming to terms with the idea that perhaps Ambra and I were destined for a different path than the rest of our sisters. And as long as we were on that path together, I was at peace. In the beginning, each boat had made its recipient feel like the exception to the rule. But now Ambra and I had become the exceptions, and I found some pride in that.

We settled into a daily rhythm together. I walked the beach in the early morning, watching the sun cast deep purples and pinks across the canvas of the sky, while Ambra slept. We took our meals together, but I often handled breakfast alone to let her sleep. Ambra usually trekked into the forest around midday to scavenge, and she never ceased to surprise me with a small token, like a bird-shaped rock or a handful of wild raspberries, when she returned. We learned the other's ebb and flow as well as we knew the ocean's tides. Some days we joked, some days we snipped, and some days we spent in silence. Our moods could shift as easily as the breeze. But the one constant was that the other was never far if we needed something, anything—a hand, a hug, a heart.

Our living arrangement had been makeshift for some time. Ambra and I had put off investing too much into our downsized camp because we had assumed that it was only temporary—that sooner or later we would be leaving it behind. But when the weather turned warm and the breeze shifted to the east, we started to add flourishes. It was never something we spoke about—it just happened.

We started building an ornate door for our hut from palm fronds, which we then reinforced with branches and layered with bark. We decorated it with swirls of braided reeds and colored shells and created a latch to hold it shut against the coaxing of the breeze. The day we hung it, we must have opened and shut it a thousand times, admiring our handiwork, testing out the latch against the other's mock attempts to open it. When we retired for the night, the door securely latched behind us, I slept better than I had in a long time.

When I awoke the next morning, I found myself alone in the hut. I stretched luxuriantly, rubbed my eyes, and then with a groan, hoisted myself to my feet and slipped out the door into the sun. I found Ambra sitting on the sand about thirty yards away, her back toward me, looking out to the horizon.

You let me sleep too late! I called.

When Ambra turned to face me, I saw that her cheeks were glistening.

What's wrong? I asked.

Her eyes were so full of sorrow that her pupils looked like tiny islands surrounded by the saltwater of her tears. She gestured toward the direction she had been looking.

There, amidst a pink sky warming into orange, was a faint shape, so far off, it was hard to put into focus, but a shape nonetheless. And with each passing moment, it grew just a tiny bit bigger.

I knelt in the sand beside her, grabbed her hand, and squeezed. We sat there for a long time, our fingers locked. Yesterday, we'd had all the time in the world, and today, our time was almost up.

It would be several hours before the boat made it to shore, so Ambra and I spent the morning building up our stores—we filled every gourd we could find with fresh water from the inland stream, we chopped firewood until our hands bled, we gathered as many fruits and nuts as we could find, we braided bark into coils and coils of twine. We had decided long ago that the majority of what we gathered would not be for the boat, but for the one left behind. The one who would now have to do everything alone. We did not yet know who that would be.

I imagined both scenarios as I had done many times before—that the boat was for me, and that it wasn't. I studied each imagining, looking for hints of which one would turn out to be true. I feared that if I were able to imagine the boat being for me in too much detail, it wouldn't come to be. That to be real, the experience couldn't be fully known until it happened. But of course I wanted that boat to be for me. I had seen, time and again, that it was always easier to leave than to be left behind. For the person who left, everything changed all at once, and with that came limitless possibilities. For the person who stayed, there was only loss and trying to fill the gaping hole the other had left. With each departure, our individual burdens grew larger and harder to bear—cooking, hunting, gathering, patching, sharpening, chopping. That was why it was so important for us to build up our supplies—to remove whatever burden we could from the one left behind, and also from the conscience of the one leaving, at least for a little while.

When the boat came close enough to haul in, Ambra and I linked hands and waded into the waves together. *Let's not look yet, OK?* she asked. I nodded. We kept our eyes only on the curved bow, refusing to glance anywhere near the seat, though the pull to do so was strong. It was a large canoe, made of polished red cedar. We pulled it ashore, kept our backs to it, then walked a few feet from the water so that we were far enough away that it wasn't possible to see the carving even if we tried. We sat down next to each other on the sand and watched the waves lap at the stern.

No matter who it's for, it's a good thing, I said to Ambra, trying to convince both her and myself that this was true. *One of us will make the journey now, and then the final boat will be along soon enough for the other.*

But what if it's not? asked Ambra, picking at the calluses on her hands.

It is, I said. *It has to be. And it's important we believe that, both of us, no matter whose name is on that seat.*

I wish we could just sit here forever, said Ambra. *Not knowing feels safer than knowing.*

I know, I said, putting my hand over hers. *But we really shouldn't delay. We can't afford another storm.*

She sat there for a moment, took a few measured breaths, then squeezed my hand to let me know she was ready.

We walked slowly toward the canoe together, my hand clasped in hers, my pulse pounding in my ears. Together, we read the carving in the seat:

Ambra

We both collapsed onto the wet sand, crying against the other's shoulder, Ambra, I imagine, in relief, but it was grief that brought me to my knees.

If other send-offs had been a shout, my goodbye with Ambra was a whisper. There weren't any words left that we had not already spoken to each other over the past six seasons of our shared life together. *I love you*, she whispered. *Stay safe.* As I hugged her for the last time, I wondered if it would be the last time I hugged anyone.

I'll be fine, I told her, though I really wasn't sure about that, or anything for that matter. *Don't be sad*, I whispered. *Be happy. My boat will be along soon enough.*

It will, she said, gripping my shoulders and looking straight into my eyes. *And I will be waiting for you when it does.*

I pulled her into a tight embrace, desperate to hold onto her just a little bit longer, desperate to believe everything we were saying.

See you soon, I said, choking on the last word before pulling away. Quickly wiping the tears from my eyes, I helped her settle into the canoe, then started pulling it into the water, as if this were something of my choosing.

I stood there for a long time, watching Ambra slowly shrink against the vast backdrop of the sky. She kept her eyes on me, her back to the blazing sun, but soon enough, she became just another shimmer of light on the water. I had been through so many heart-wrenching goodbyes. I didn't know how to feel about this one being my last.

The following days and nights became both fuller and emptier. I had so much more to do alone, and the physical exhaustion wore me down, like water cutting stone. Without my sisters, without Ambra, it felt as though my soul had left my body. As the days turned to weeks and the weeks to a full season, exhaustion took over my mind as well. I had not been prepared to carry the full weight of the world on my shoulders each day, only to fall into a restless sleep under a lonely moon each night. I ripped the roof off my hut so I could see the evening sky and pretend that each of my sisters was one of the stars looking down on me, trying to convince myself I was not as alone as I felt. I talked to the gulls each morning when I went to gather mussels and left piles of algae for the blue crab I often saw near the tide pools and had named Fribi. By then, he was more important to me as a friend than as food.

One morning, when I awoke to the glare of sunshine peeking through the hut walls behind my closed lids, I could not bring myself to get up. Not only was I empty of energy, but the sense of purpose that had forced me out of bed each day was gone. I could not bring myself to sit up, much less to leave the shelter. I wanted to hide from everything. The world felt too harsh, my skin too raw. It was too hard. And so, I stayed holed up there for several days. From time to time, I dribbled a few droplets of water onto my tongue, but I could not bring myself to eat. I found that I preferred feeling the pang of hunger over the void of loneliness that both resided in my gut. I did not fetch water nor gather food. I did not mend my hut nor set out my fish traps. I did not chop wood nor build or tend the fire. It was all I could do to just exist.

When I finally exhausted my water supply, thirst drew me outside my hut for the first time in days. I was weak and tired and hungry. The sand felt rough against my feet, the wind stinging to my cheeks, and I squinted my eyes against the blinding light of the sun. As I began to pile kindling to start a fire, I glanced at the sun climbing over the horizon to assess how late it was. And that's when I saw it. The faint shadow at the edge of the world where the sea met the sky. I shook my head and blinked my eyes, assuming it was just a transient spot in my vision from the glare of daylight. But when I looked again, it was still there, albeit perhaps just a little bit larger than it had been before. As I continued to coax the neglected fire back to life, I could feel the faint embers of hope reawakening in my body, too. Once the fire was burning again and I had refilled my water supply, I nibbled on nuts and seeds from my stockpile. I had been hungry for so long that I no longer felt it. Silently, I thanked my past self for storing all that extra wood and food when I'd still had the energy to do so during better days. I plunged into the waves over and over again, letting the cool water reawaken the senses I'd been trying to dull. It was overwhelming to feel again, but it was also invigorating. I didn't know what the day would bring, but I knew it would bring something, and that was enough.

As I returned slowly to my normal routine, resting in the cool shade of the banyan trees when I felt myself growing light-headed between chores, I kept my eyes on the horizon, on the shape that was slowly growing closer. If that dark blob was not my boat, I was in no condition to withstand the crushing disappointment of that discovery. I was too fragile for hope of any kind.

By early evening, I realized there was something off about the object headed to shore. Although it was long and narrow, there was something wrong with the shape. The silhouette was lopsided and irregular, and it seemed to just be floating versus moving with intent. My stomach clenched into a small fist of dread. I set off to gather firewood in the hills for a couple hours, which would obstruct my vision of whatever was heading toward me, though it did nothing to slow the tsunami of thoughts and feelings churning through my brain.

The sun was just about to disappear into the sea when the shape came close enough to see. It was not a boat, but rather, the trunk of a dead tree with long, gnarled roots dangling like octopus tentacles. The debris of faraway lives and worlds that I knew now I would never get to see. The day had brought me not a boat, or an escape, or a grand new destiny. It had brought me soggy firewood that still needed to be chopped. As I waded into the surf to drag it ashore, away from the greedy fingers of the tide, I felt all the anger and frustration and disappointment rising up inside me. I grabbed one of the roots too roughly and it broke off in my hand. Cursing, I grabbed the tree again as the waves carried it onto the sand.

Why? I yelled to the sky.

Taking a running start, I rushed up to the tree and started kicking it, over and over again.

Why am I still here? Why me? I screamed as I ripped off one of the roots and began beating the tree trunk with it. *What more do you want from me?*

Again and again, I brought the thick gnarled root down on the trunk, pulverizing the wet bark. And with each blow, a small bit of me burst, releasing the yearning that had been trapped inside of me, that had been denied for so long. I swung and swung until my entire body ached, and I could no longer feel my arm. Heaving, I fell back against the wet sand, my heart pounding, the breeze licking the salt from the tears and sweat on my face.

Why not me? I whispered, and then the world went black.

When I came to, I felt lighter than I had in months. All this time, I'd been going through the motions, pretending I was fine in hopes of not jeopardizing my own worthiness for a boat to come, when all I really wanted to do was scream at the sky until it answered me. And now that I had, I felt better, even if I hadn't received an answer. Everything was out in the open now, I could stop pretending, and there was some relief in that.

The tree trunk lay where I had left it, though it looked more weathered after the beating I had given it the day before. In the places where the blows had demolished the cocoa-colored bark, a lighter, smoother wood peeked through. And it was at that moment that I realized I *had* gotten my answer. This tree trunk may not be the boat I had expected or imagined, but that did not mean it wasn't my boat.

A tendril of newfound purpose sprouted within me, and I started to prepare for the work ahead. I filled every gourd I could find with water so I would stay hydrated, set the fish traps so I would have something for dinner, and most importantly, I sharpened the stone of my ax. When I finished grinding the blade to my liking, I began the arduous process of removing all the bark. Unlike last night, each blow to the tree filled me with excitement and possibility. With each whack, I was a step closer to creating the boat I had dreamed about for so long. And the best part was, the only thing I had to wait for was me, and me alone.

Two days later, the tree lay naked on the sand, the honey-colored wood feeling the rays of the sun on its pale skin for the first time. I sank down into the sand and leaned against it, tilted my head to feel the breeze across my face, felt the warmth of the wood seeping into my back. This was my boat, and just like with my sisters, the timing could not be rushed. It would be ready when it was ready, and hopefully I would be ready by then, too.

The hard work of carving my boat gave my life new shape and focus. Unlike the daily labors I'd been shouldering alone for so long, this work was not about maintenance or survival. Instead, this work was about creating change and building a future—a future I had once so readily dreamed of and nearly given up on.

Each morning, I worked in earnest until either the boat or my body said no more. Each night, I fell asleep exhausted but satisfied. However, I would be lying if I did not admit my impatience. But I knew not to rush. I needed it to float, to remain steady, to be able to withstand rough seas and high winds. If I hurried the process or took shortcuts, the only place I would end up when I finally left the island was the bottom of the sea.

If I'm honest, I was scared, too. I was scared to leave the only home I'd ever known. I was scared of what I'd find out there in that wide expanse of ocean.

Over the following weeks, as the wood became less and less treelike and more and more boatlike, it became harder and harder to contain both my excitement and my fears. After all, who was I to judge when the boat was finally good enough, when I had never been judged as good enough?

I found perfection to be a useful tactic for stalling—buffing out every blemish, sanding down every splinter. Meanwhile, the seat remained as empty and clean as a rock face.

The time finally came when the work was done. I don't know how I knew; I just did. I woke up one morning and understood that what I had done was enough. That anything else would be a waste of time, of energy, of resources. My boat was as seaworthy as it would ever be. I had checked and rechecked it from every angle and view and even performed a float test the day before. It was time to start preparing for my departure and saying my goodbyes.

There would be no elaborate send-off, no feast, no laughter-filled day of sisterhood. But that did not mean I had to forego the celebration. In fact, I deserved it that much more, to have accomplished this feat of labor and love on my own versus having it handed to me.

I decided to celebrate through some finishing touches. I spent the morning affixing shells of pale blue and dusty pink and bone white to the bow with sap that I then hardened into place with fire. I stained the edges purple with the juice of berries, then draped garlands of white flowers over them. When I had finished, I stopped to survey my work, my eyes coming to rest on the smooth, unblemished seat in the middle. I had always assumed that the final step would be to carve my name into it, just like the others had had their names carved into theirs. But looking at it now, I realized I didn't want or need my name there. It was not the biggest or most beautiful boat, but it was mine in a way that the others' boats had not been for them. And it was mine in a way no other boat could ever be.

I decided to finish the day by preparing my supplies before spending one last night in my hut with my sisters smiling down at me from the night sky, and then slip into the sea at dawn.

It was a fitful night of sleep. Though my body was exhausted, my mind was churning with everything I would miss about the island. The rainbow sunsets. The whisper of the wind through the trees. The soft crash and retreat of the waves. The sound of raindrops falling on the palm fronds. The sweet juice of a ripe cherimoya breaking in my mouth. The shrieks of the seagulls flying overhead. All of these things were as much a part of me as the freckles on my arms, the hair on my head, the beat of my own heart, and yet I would soon be leaving them behind.

I don't think I slept, really, just dozed on and off throughout the night, the familiar lullaby of the surf unable to soothe me. I finally got up just as the sun was beginning to peek its rosy head beneath the blue-black blanket of sky. Gathering the fruit pits I had been saving since I first began working on my boat, I walked to the freshwater stream on the island one last time, casting the pits into the forest as I went, seeding bounty for the life that would remain. After each toss, I bowed my head in gratitude for everything the island had provided for me. I pressed my hands to the trunks of the trees, their bark cool against my touch, absorbing my warmth. I filled my now-empty basket with long strips of seaweed that had snagged along the shore. When I reached the tidepools that Fribi liked to frequent, I arranged them in a pile so that he would have a feast of his own. I waited for a bit to see if he would come out, but it was still too early, too dark.

Goodbye, my friend, I whispered.

When I reached camp again, I began to transfer the supplies I'd been stockpiling into the boat—the sleeping mat, the gourds of fresh water, the fruits and nuts, my fishing net, coils of rope and twine, herbs and tinctures for ailments. Once finished, I walked over to the hut that I had shared with Ambra, peeled a piece of braided reed from the door we had decorated together, and tied it snugly around my wrist, just below the coral bracelet that Galena had made me so long ago. Galena and Ambra. The beginning and the end.

I thought of each of my sisters, how this island had once been ours, and now there would be no one—just traces of what we'd left behind, and even then, that would all eventually be washed or blown away. But what we'd shared here mattered—it had been and would always be our home, the place where we'd learned to love and fight and laugh and thrive, together.

I break off a branch from a nearby tree, and slowly write each of their names in the sand—*Galena, Addy, Cheyene, Mendha, Eula, Kyli, Rubie, Esme, Rhea, Liann, Lynet, Dayal, Tarrah, Ambra.*

The last name I write in the sand is my own.

And so it is. And so it is. And so it is.

I head back toward the boat and begin pulling it toward the water, singing softly under my breath:

Oh sister, may the sun shine bright …

The water is cool against my legs and the outgoing tide pulls me and the boat forward, as though beckoning us to follow it.

And when you hear the breeze through leaves …

Once I get the boat past the break line, I haul myself into it, steady myself on the seat, and pick up the oars.

Oh sister, may the sea stay calm …

With each pull, the island retreats just a little bit more. I cannot tell whether the droplets on my face are from the spray of the saltwater, the trek of my tears, or both.

And when you hear the waves at night …

When the wind picks up, I take a brief opportunity to rest, letting it carry me in the direction of its choosing. Perhaps I will find something better than this island, the only home I've ever known. Perhaps I will find something worse. Perhaps I will find Ambra and my other sisters. Perhaps I will find nothing at all.

I lift my face to feel the warmth of the rising sun. It is the golden moment in which there is a boat, and it is beautiful, and it is for me. In every direction, there is nothing but sea, sky, and the brilliant shimmer of possibility.

Sara Moore Wagner

Self-Portrait as Buffalo Bill's Best Horse

I loved a man who drew me with feathers
in my hair, who wore his limbs like strands
of beads. They moved him and moved me
to the basin of his chest where I'd dip
to drink. I'd eat cereal from his chest,
bowl dented in where I could just make
out the slow beat of him, how like running,
sinewy. In the stories, a girl is transformed
and what's left but a bark or low, Io
opening her mouth to find she is a cow,
has been lowered to the earth, glances
into the ocean to see the sideways movement
of her jaw, grass in the teeth. When I said
undo me, this is what I wanted, to be free
of that great God who says what a girl can
do with her body, to be inside the man
I loved, to let him ride me into his own,
particular sunset. *Let me be sunset*, I said,
let me be particles of dust in his eye.
And God, like he does, gave me
the image of myself long-faced and limbed,
brushed and oiled and fitted with iron
shoes I stomp across the landscape.
When I open my mouth, the neigh
of me unshapes my face and it's almost
humanlike, they say. I'm an absence
and propulsion, a sonic gesture, a bow
down to the haunches to release

the rider. I am tucking myself into
the night—let the groomers come
and the flies come, let them decorate me
with daisies, parade me. I release
every last bit of what made me
girl, what makes me his.
I trade the lack for rhythm,
beating of hooves in a dirt-strewn
amphitheater, the crack of peanuts,
whips. I was not always like this.

Angie Macri

Obsessive/Compulsive

An only child is a danger, especially a daughter
because she is the apple
of her father's eye, because she likes dancing.
She sings to herself without mirrors
and dust rises in ghosts
to join her. Although she never
sees this at first. Only her father, watching.
She walks the road and dust follows
and joy falls in her wake. He is worried.
That phase falls heavy whenever it pleases
and she hasn't learned yet
it has nothing to do with her
or his promises
to god. A vow, he calls it. Others, a bargain.
Neither the devil
nor god enter into these deals,
but men persist in them. If you let me win,
I will give you the first thing I see next.
I will cut its throat, set it on fire.
She grows to sense she causes trouble
by even existing. She should disappear
in mountains, forests,
fire. The ghosts invite her.
The god doesn't interfere, expecting
both father and daughter to know better.

Ma Hua

Autumn Harvest

On the rooftop, warm corn kernels strum sunrays,
where underneath, a forgotten stable lies.
By weariness, an old gray mare dozes off
and dreams among crushed stalks and fecal-mixed mud.
Dreams that it becomes a small and lean rider.

Translated from the Chinese by Winnie Zeng

Chelsea Stickle

The Psychic Pretends to Read Tarot Cards

For months Lizzy had been having these pulsing headaches—
"episodes" her mother called them—where she tasted things she
wasn't eating, felt things that weren't touching her, heard words and
smelled scents no one else did, and saw pictures that moved in her
head like an old flip-book that got stuck sometimes. Lizzy can't
control it. Her mom told her that her overactive imagination would
get her in trouble. She was desperate for her daughter to be normal,
so they could be the same. When Anna's mom calls Lizzy's mom
for a sleepover, Lizzy's mom is thrilled—signs of a social life!—and
Lizzy can't fight her when she gets like that, so she goes limp, doesn't
even think about whether she wants to go or what that would mean.
And that's how Lizzy and her Ninja Turtles sleeping bag ended up in
Anna the Bedwetter's moldy basement fingering tarot cards.

Anna slips the tarot cards out of her blue-checked dress pocket
like they're contraband. There's chocolate smudged in the corner of
her mouth from the fresh-from-the-oven Ghriradelli triple chocolate
box brownies her mom made for them after dinner. Spoonfuls of
brownie straight from the pan. The girls giggling over nothing, high
off the sugar.

"The cards are my mom's," Anna whispers conspiratorially. Now
they have a secret. Secrets bond you. "But I don't know how to read
them."

Of course she would expect Lizzy the Witchy Weirdo to know
how. A couple weeks ago, everyone's bagged lunches had gotten
ransacked by the science teacher's snake food: live mice. When the
girls were the first back from PE, Lizzy blocked the door and asked
if Anna would go to the water fountain with her. A weird request but

---

24

Anna nodded. The class's mean girl went inside instead. Her scream was heard in every room.

"How'd you know?" Anna asked. No one ever cared about her. No one ever looked out for her.

Lizzy wiped her mouth with the back of her hand. "Know what?"

If Anna the Bedwetter wanted to dabble in the occult, Lizzy could, too. "I can read them."

"Really?" Anna's features rise. "Can you give me a reading?"

Anna picks the three that "speak" to her. Lizzy hesitates to ask if Anna actually *heard* anything, but stops when she hears her mother asking why she can't make friends like her baby sister.

The three cards: Seven of Swords, The Tower, The Devil.

The movement of The Tower catches Lizzy's attention and her hands dart for a closer look. On the card, people fall out tower windows, hit the ground, and spurt blood. Then it starts all over again. Lizzy's never seen anything like this before. As the thought hits her, she's sucked into a scene she doesn't understand.

The feeling of being scrubbed pink and clean, like there was nothing grimy or dirty left. Tongue slips across fresh, minty teeth. Mother says goodnight. Dad stays. Her body seizes and the organs scramble to get away. "When your mom goes to bed, your dad stays," Lizzy says.

He gets into Anna's bed, and Lizzy can feel his rough fingers under her thin floral rayon pajamas getting closer and closer to the part she's supposed to protect. The Tower card drops. Lizzy descends into the fetal position with the speed of an armadillo retreating into armored ball mode. A grunt escapes her mouth. When that doesn't scare away the scene, she hums "Ob-La-Di, Ob-La-Da." She doesn't notice she's wet herself. She's still in Anna's bedroom. She doesn't know how to get out of this memory. Banging on its walls doesn't work, screaming doesn't work, begging for help doesn't work, so she pretends she's somewhere else. A good memory. One of hers.

Freshly baked chocolate chip cookies—when she pulls them apart and the chocolate can't stand to be separated so it maintains bridges until they collapse. Licking the middle to catch the escaping chocolate and missing so it drips down her chin. Grammy wiping her face with a damp napkin. Gently scolding her with that whinnying laugh she has. Her sister brags about her cleanliness. Grammy winks and says, "Sometimes you have to make a mess."

Lizzy's eye snaps open and she's back in the basement. It worked. When she registers her pee-soaked pants, she glances up at Anna, who's weeping big blobs onto her dress. Near the hem, Anna's fists bunch the cloth and twist it in different directions. Her mouth is open since her snot-filled nose isn't really useful.

For the first time she and Anna understand each other. "I'm sorry," Lizzy says. "I didn't know that would happen—." She moves to hug Anna, but Anna backs away like she's the monster in a horror movie.

"What's wrong with you?" Anna yells. "You—you're sick. You're gross."

Guilt nips at Lizzy's heels. She can't change anything that's already happened. "I want to go home."

They can't meet each other's eyes. They never speak again. Anna's mother doesn't find The Tower card under one of the basement chairs. Never even notices it's missing. In her father's looming face, Anna sees Lizzy, her lost hope and something else new and lonely. The knowledge that someone knows and nothing's changed.

Once Lizzy changes her clothes, she waits on the front step for her dad to fold his arms around her until she's ready to let go. But her mom arrives in a black coat over pajamas and a crease so deep between her eyebrows that Lizzy wonders when she'll crack open and spill all her secrets.

In the car she screams at Lizzy about how she's a worthless freak. Lizzy knows the rest of the speech detailing how no one will ever love her if this is what she does to people willing to take a chance on her. *You're broken, broken, broken.* When Lizzy reaches for a positive memory to combat it, they slip like smoke between her fingers and dissipate into the ether.

Shawn Nocher

Vernal Communion

He relies on her to save him. But every time he pumps a dream into his arm he is disappointed in her again. He is squatting at the edge of a muddy pond. The sun is warm, the water still except for the squiggling at the edges. In this dream place, words are things he has a feeling for, but no mastery over. They wiggle in and out of his brain but are especially slippery when he has much to say. He cannot name the flagellates at the water's edge, but he would like to hold them in his hand, feel the tickle of them. He has all the time in the world, time to watch them change into another creature wholly unlike what they are now—would like to know the magic of it. The spring pond is an alphabet soup of lowercase frogs.

Oh, she would have something to say about this. She'd be angry, maybe even *herstorical*. He can find this word because it is theirs. He made it up the first time she screeched. Enough is enough!

When he rose from their bed in the early morning, the taste of her still in his mouth, he had been surprised by the bumping up of another longing. It hadn't occurred to him at all to want for anything other than the slip of her skin against his. Until it did.

When he texted his guy, there was a strange satisfaction that came from the act of sliding the phone from his pocket, all the while watching the back of her through the crack in the bathroom door. She had a baby shower to go to, a luncheon in the city. When she came from the bathroom, he had tucked the phone in his pocket, smiled at her, at the blue of the dress she wore that changed the color of her eyes, and she swirled her back to him. Wordlessly asking him to run the zipper. The fine line of her spine that had curled to him the night before disappearing beneath its track.

☾

He isn't bothered by his inability to name the things around him, the crispy-creamy spirals that slime the muddy banks, the jeweled wing-broaches that dip and tickle the surface of the looking glass, the arrowheads that dart the sky. He is confused by this failing, but not alarmed. He thinks if he tried harder, if he were so inclined, he could dig the words out, shiny them up and hang them precisely in the sky—but why bother, when he is just as happy—happier, in fact—with the raw feel of them.

Long time no see, said his guy. He wanted to tell him it's been sixty-seven days, sixty-seven goddamn days and isn't that enough? But his brain quickened. With so much time in between, he has forgotten the ruin of it all. Thinks instead that this is the reward for his efforts. He has tamed the beast and will ride the swell of it. And at the end of the day, he will stable the monster. Another unfettered flight in the books. That was the plan.

Here comes the willow, her dress so blue it fades into the sky and he wonders if she is only the pigment of his imagination. She is pounding through the furrows, throws up the subjects at her feet so that she moves in a cloud of animation, sending up scatters of the words he tastes and swallows, flutterflies and glasslippers and a single fat pheasant that rises in a clump, spreads its cloak and swifts low across the field.

He has a sudden need to be lower to the ground, lower than the squat he is in allows. Deep in the earth. Why, she asks. It is a herstorical question that she will ask again and again until it sounds like one long word, like the incessant night-barking of a dog that becomes a howl. And still, on this sunny day that he has ridden, the moon hangs, unfazed, somewhere.

If he had words right now, he would explain to her the draw of the ritual, the anticipation that he had savored, driving home slowly, parking the truck so perfectly in the ruts of last night's rain that it looked like he had never left. The way the heat crept up the spoon, the pumping of his tired veins which, by the way, didn't look so bad anymore.

☾

The beast has dumped him to the ground. His mouth is filling with the coppery taste of earth.

If he could dig out the sorrowing language, he would ask again for forgiveness between the two of them, and he knows the graveyard feeling of it, but cannot uncover the words. It is only a too-late place. He would ask her to sit, wordlessly, in the too-late place with him. Suffer the feudility of his request.

Luke Rolfes

Ethan, Deep in the Collapsed Mine

The mine had collapsed at two-thirty in the morning. The other workers, also trapped, called to Ethan. It was time, they yelled, to huddle together in the darkness, to ride out the terrible, lightless storm. But Ethan decided that wasn't his way.

Instead, he ventured deeper into the earth, crawling along the mine's floor—a place he imagined first as cold but then warmer as he descended toward thermal heat.

The crust of the planet is somewhere around forty-four miles thick. He had read that once. The Kora Superdeep Borehole near the Barents Sea was the lowest hole ever dug. A Russian expedition. And the Russians had only reached a depth of seven miles.

Hell could be down there, below him. The Indian Ocean. One wayward pickaxe could open a fissure that would fill the entire mine with magma.

He couldn't hear his co-workers anymore. Their prayers and pleadings in the void. They'd given up on him. To them, he had already died. Radios didn't work at this depth. Ethan had gone manic in the darkness, they'd likely say, if they were retrieved.

Up top, a graveyard filled the outskirts of town behind the Casey's General Store. That's where they buried the miners who didn't make it. Or artifacts of those who disappeared. Six feet underground. Deep enough to decompose but at least a mile above where Ethan sat in the collapsed mine, trying to remember how his mine connected to another mine (an older, forgotten mine) in the way that all water is connected to all water.

It's OK, he thought, if I don't make it out. He promised he would forgive himself if he couldn't solve the impossible riddle in front of him.

☾

It was a couple hours (or days) later when Ethan encountered the mine rabbit. The rabbit didn't call itself a mine rabbit. That's what Ethan called it. Instead, it called itself a cave rabbit. Rabbits knew little about mines, but they knew a cave when they saw one.

"My friend, it's not safe for us down here," said Ethan. "We need to get out."

"It is incredibly safe down here," said the mine rabbit.

After a while, Ethan admitted, "I can't see at all anymore. I can't see you. I can't see anything."

"I have red eyes, probably," said the mine rabbit. "I have gray fur and a white belly. I like carrots, which make my eyes better and redder. Though I have only tasted carrots once. I lived in a yard, years ago. Children fed carrots to me. Their father brought home a terrible dog, and then I no longer lived in a yard."

Ethan removed his gloves and felt the walls again. Hardness, sediment, and then more hardness. There was an old tunnel around somewhere. An escape shaft dug back when the mine was young. He had never found it before, but some of his co-workers claimed it existed. It needed to exist.

"Rabbit," he said. "Do you know a way out of the darkness?"

"Yes and no," said the mine rabbit.

"I don't understand."

"Once I walked a long time. Through different passages. And then I found myself in the sun and wind. That is what I know."

Ethan reached out in the blackness, toward the mine rabbit's voice. "Can I pet you? I want to make certain you are real."

"I am no one's pet."

Through endless night, Ethan and the mine rabbit walked. Several times in their journey he thought the creature had abandoned him, but then he would hear the soft thump of its hops, and he knew it was still there, following or guiding him. He wondered if he reached a certain level of hunger, would he consider eating the mine rabbit to prolong his survival? And what would something taste like in complete darkness, on the brink of starvation? Would it be better? Spiritual? What if, in his confusion, he circled back and happened upon his co-workers? Would they steal the mine rabbit for their own?

The thought of his impending death haunted him. His canteen was only two-thirds full of water, and he knew that he could only last so long down here, perhaps less than a week, and the more he thought about his end, the more he felt emptiness in the pit of his stomach. It was better to not think of anything except the task in front of him.

"Do you have a family?" said Ethan. "My family will never believe I am lost."

"I have created others."

"Here's a funny thought. The last thing I did above ground," said Ethan, "was go to a city council meeting. My wife is on the city council. She's a great civil servant, at being involved. There was a mandate from the mayor that the city council voted to overturn. The people in the audience cheered when it happened. I don't know why they cheered. They even brought signs. I don't think they understood what the mandate was supposed to do. But I remember my wife crying in the car on the way home. The mandate had been her idea in the first place. She didn't want to talk to me, or talk about the city forum. When I tried to console her, she said, 'Just let me cry.'"

The mine rabbit didn't say anything.

"Don't you want to know her name? It's Nicole, by the way. Don't you want to know anything about me?"

"Yes."

"What do you want to know?"

The mine rabbit said, "What is your mate's name?"

"I told you. Her name is Nicole. She's on the city council. She's probably up there still crying about the mandate, not realizing I'm gone. She's probably starting up an episode of *Criminal Minds* on Netflix. Not knowing the tremendous danger her husband is in."

"Are you in tremendous danger?"

"Yes."

"But it's incredibly safe down here."

"Stop saying that."

The mine rabbit was silent again. Then it said, "I know what I would like to ask. Do you think Nicole would rather have, for a mate, someone who lived underground for many years, or someone who lived in a tree, or someone who moved from one place to the next, sleeping in a different building every day of its life?"

☾

There was little to be done after the city council meeting when the townspeople in the parking lot confronted the two nurses who had testified about the efficacy of the mandate. Under the haze of streetlights, the people in the parking lot came at the nurses with camera phones, chirping and barking with flecks of spit and empty, vague threats. "You are not welcome here," they said. "We know who you are. Everyone knows who you are. We *know*." There was a sure-handedness to the way they spoke—almost arrogant—as if it had suddenly dawned on them that they could get away with telling someone "I want to kill you" by saying, "I wish somebody would kill you."

Later that night, one nurse called Nicole and explained to her what had happened. Ethan heard his wife say into the phone, "You cannot be serious." And then, after a few moments, "What's wrong with us? What's wrong with people?" And then, several minutes after that, when she hung up and set the phone atop the nightstand, Ethan expected her to break down again, as she had done in the car, but instead she pointed at the television and said, "Turn that up."

The Olympics were on NBC. Track and field. Ethan hadn't really been watching, but he followed his wife's fingers to the screen—thinly muscled bodies in motion. Uniforms the color of flags. Without thinking, he increased the volume and slid the remote across the bedsheets.

"This is the steeplechase," said Nicole. "Nobody understands it."

At some point, sleep overtook them both.

In the morning, his wife was gone before he woke. Ethan's keys were nowhere to be found. A groggy scramble through the house, turning in and out the pockets in each of his jeans and coats. He checked the bathroom sink, his car's ignition, the cushions of the love seat. He thought for a minute he would have to call in sick because he would rather skip than show up late and get written up.

But then, when all felt lost, he spied his keys splayed underneath the kitchen table. He had no idea how they had gotten there.

"And if I wouldn't have seen those keys, everything would be different," he told the mine rabbit. "I would have been aboveground, watching this all unfold on TV. Eating whatever I wanted. Taking hot showers. Even baths. Can you believe that?"

"I can," said the mine rabbit.

Ethan sighed. A long sigh—one that empties the lungs. A feeling of fatigue spread from his core to his fingertips and toes. He had slept recently, he thought, for a few minutes. Or maybe he had slept long ago. Either way, he felt ready to sleep again.

"Rabbit," he said. "I might need a favor from you. If I die, will you tell Nicole what happened to me?"

"You are going to die."

"That's what I fear. There's no way out of the mine."

"You are going to die."

"That's what I said."

"Yes."

Ethan continued forward, but after several dozen steps his chest grew tight. His breath became difficult to catch, as if he were breathing through a straw. He bent over in the darkness, hand on his sternum, and took a long drink from the canteen's precious water. Maybe he was deeper beneath the earth than he thought, in a place where oxygen was scarce. Maybe he was sleep deprived and having a panic attack. Or a heart attack. He called into the emptiness, "I might take a break. Please."

Kneeling on the cold ground, Ethan scooted backwards until his shoulders rested against the wall. There was no one near, he realized. Seated in oblivion. A black nothingness and quietness in each direction. Another human had never felt so far away.

The rabbit was still with him, though. He was certain of that. The mine felt differently when the creature was close.

After a few minutes of slow, controlled breathing, his heart rate diminished. The light-headedness faded.

"There," he said in a soft voice.

And then, forty-five seconds later, he said more confidently, "There. Now I feel better. This whole ordeal is very stressful. I've always imagined something like this would be stressful. But I just didn't know. How could you know?"

The mine rabbit crept closer, so close Ethan swore he felt whiskers brush his arm.

More time passed. Mornings, afternoons, evenings. Ethan began to name things, to convince himself in the darkness that they were real. This is dirt, he would say. This is water in my mouth, giving life. This is a wall that I can touch with my forearm. This is walking, what

I am doing. I am walking toward an exit that exists, somewhere in front or maybe above me.

"This is me. This is us," Ethan said after a long period of silence. "We are deep in the collapsed mine. This is where we are."

"Collapsed mind," said the mine rabbit.

"No, mine."

"What is mine?"

"Mine. What has collapsed."

"The mind has collapsed."

"Never mind," said Ethan, more than a little annoyed.

He thought, for a moment, that he would have laughed about this conversation were he aboveground. The ridiculousness of it. Here, in the deep, humor seemed arbitrary.

Why would the rabbit contradict him? Why would it not just follow along? Why did it refuse to help or lead him out of the darkness?

The rabbit could see, he reasoned. It must be able to. Rabbits, through millions of years of evolution, have rods and cones and corneas that can adapt to the darkness.

Only one explanation made sense. The mine rabbit was following him out of curiosity. Waiting for him to die.

Ethan didn't have the energy for anger. He wanted, momentarily, to say something hurtful, but when he opened his mouth, he cried out a name into the darkness. It was likely Nicole, his wife's name, but, at the same time, it could be almost anyone's. His mother, maybe. He would, for instance, love to see the foreman now. Or one of the bosses. Or a paramedic. A person with a shovel. Children with runny noses, playing in the dirt. A discarded flashlight with a weak beam. A map. A candy bar. A bottle of Gatorade.

He cried again and again, a name into the darkness. There was desperation in his voice. The ground swallowed the words as soon as they left his lips. But he couldn't stop himself. It was the beginning of the end, he realized.

He was losing control.

Another day passed. And another. It could have been the same day.

Ethan allowed himself to drink the rest of his canteen. He had been rationing, but the dryness of his throat took over, and he couldn't take his lips from the nozzle. It was erotic, gulping mouthful after mouthful of water, canteen straight above his head. But, as soon as he swallowed the last of the water, depression took over. An unconquerable sadness filled the mine.

There will be no more, he realized. The last physical comfort he would receive in his lifetime. No more cool pillows beneath his head. No warm slices of bread or steaming bowls of soup. No loving arms. No warming liquids. No nothing. Only pain and the cold rock beneath him. And whatever was standing in the way between him and eternity.

He curled his body against the wall, hugging his knees to his chest. A defeated shape in the blackness. Not actually awake. Not actually asleep. The mine rabbit sat next to his feet, twitching softly in the way rabbits do.

Rock bottom. The earth's floor beneath him was the embodiment. Dimly, he could sense it. The irony. One of the lowest people in the world dying a lowly death.

He said to the rabbit, "It was good to be with you at the end."

"It is never the end," said the rabbit.

"I believe it is."

"But there is no end to a cave that circles back on itself."

"Life is not a circle. It is a straight line. I know that now. I didn't earlier."

"It is crucial that you keep going," said the mine rabbit.

"Crucial?"

"Crucial."

"Why would it be?"

"Because," said the rabbit, "it's not the end until it is."

"You just said there wasn't an end."

"I said there is no end to a cave that circles back on itself."

Before Ethan could argue, he heard a sound. And then another sound. Faint in the darkness. Voices in the deep. Human voices. Calling out. Saying a name. His name.

And then the voices sounded again. Clearer and closer.

The other miners had found Ethan. Or maybe an emergency response team. Or Nicole and all the people on the city council had come to his rescue, hoisting shovels and pickaxes. Nicole's hair wild and covered in soot. Her face glowing like a star. It could be his ancestors calling to him from the afterlife. Or the demons of hell closing in with their long knives and fingernails. The walls were closing in. That was certain. It could be his own imagination, tricking him. Like the story of the man who thinks he escapes execution, and then it ends with him hanging there, neck snapped, from Owl Creek Bridge.

"People," he said. "Do you hear people?"

"I hear what you hear."

Ethan listened. The voices sounded closer again, or maybe farther away.

"Rabbit."

"Yes."

"Is this now the end. Or is it not the end?"

The mine rabbit didn't respond.

"Rabbit," he said again.

"Yes."

"You don't know, do you?"

The mine rabbit didn't respond.

"This is the end," said Ethan. "It has to be. If it's the end, say something. Make it worthwhile. Do you understand me?"

"I understand."

"Then if it's not the end, lead me to the voices. Let's escape this place. Forever and ever."

"You can escape. But I cannot. For one must be real to escape. And you know I am not real."

"I want to escape. I need to. Let's go. I have strength left. I feel it inside."

"Escape, then. But the escape must also be real."

Ethan yelled toward the voices. He didn't know what he yelled. A word. A name. A sound. Almost instantly the voices yelled back. And he yelled again. Back and forth, until it sounded like they said, "We are coming."

"They are coming," Ethan said.

He stood, steadying himself against the wall.

"Rabbit," he said to the darkness next to him.

"I am here."

Virgil Suárez

The Body Farm

My youngest tells me all about the body farm
experience where you go in with your human

anatomy class into a few isolated acres where
the corpses are arranged in different scenarios

and left to decompose. Inside cars, sitting under
a tree, laid down in a ravine, all decomposing.

Nature taking it's sweet time. Birds plucking
hairs with which to line nests. Flies laying eggs.

The ants who make quick work of whatever salt
resides in the lacrimal glands. Buzzards gather

rather funereal and gaunt. No shadows here.
All the students with perfume plugs in their

nostrils. I can smell it all through the phone.
What is the difference in death? One day you

blow out a candle, and the next you are no better
than mulch. My mother-in-law called it a bulb

dimming, that's the signal. And I see a man rush
into the centrifugal force of atoms colliding;

his skin blushes with the tincture of poisoned
blood. Listen, that smell right now is your own

body sending the message: last night's cabbage
and boiled boudin, relish the perfume of the living.

Kieron Walquist

Border Collie—

Death is familiar on a farm. No—all over. In the shed: fly ribbon blackened + sizzling with wings; the buck hung by its hind hooves from the rafters to drip red + dry; the bobcat we caught in a foot trap + skinned after, its coat [bunched in cockleburs] on a shelf starry with salt. In the field: a pie tin I've mixed poison in to suffocate possums from the inside; the coyote we jacklight then leave to rot like a jack-o-lantern, ribs left for vultures to guitar-pick. Death is familiar because I've made it so. Always thought I had to—for our livestock, our livelihood, a little peace of mind. But you, Sage, should've died like our pet instead of something feral. Slow + in almighty pain. Scared. How you bled + shat in our mudroom on a bed gone bare-flat. I should've grabbed the gun sooner + given you rest.

Michael Beard

Terrestrial Sequence

Dead ladybugs
dot the windowsill
of my corner office.

The sunlight shapes
a mass of caskets
from their tiny shadows.

How depressing.
How freeing.

☾

Caught in the scope
of my rifle,
a deer turns her head—

the flash of an old scar
where a bullet grazed
her neck,

an unwritten word
of her survival,
her unconquered history.

No dinner tonight.

☾

I am no hunter.

☾

It is so quiet in the moonlight
where the dark sky
loses itself.

A red oak leaf

floats calmly down the river,

and I ask it to teach me
how to ease
my sunken stars.

The sky's edge
is so much like
a pocket—

it swallows everything
in the wash.

☾

I want
to play dead
like a dog
working
for a treat,

or a cat
who just wants
to sleep
in someone else's
bed for the night.

Rebecca Bernard

Witness

My husband called to me from the kitchen, "There's a body in the backyard."

Only, he had said bunny, not body. I was in bed. This was early, but the promise of a body got me moving. I twisted myself out of the sheets, the yellow summer comforter, and I came into the kitchen.

"There," he said. "Look." He pointed out the window above the kitchen sink, and there it was. A little bunny. A bunny's body.

I thought about telling him what I thought he had said—that here was a death for me to witness—but I said nothing. I watched the bunny eat a blade of grass. Then it hopped. Then it ate another blade of grass. Its nose twitched. I was far away, I was in the kitchen, but I could see this much.

I thought, what have I wanted to see in my life that wasn't this?

Then I wondered, what is it that empties this word "body" of life?

I looked at my husband, thinking to ask him for an answer, but he was so earnest, gazing out the window at the bunny, that I said nothing. We stood there like that for a few minutes watching the bunny eat. Then it hopped away.

The truth is, I have never seen a body without life. My mother—I saw her dying but not dead. The body lingers after death; it has no choice. But I couldn't wait. I had my life to live. School, the grocery store, a promise of a first kiss.

My sister stayed till the end. *It was her body*, my sister told me, *but she was gone.* All that was left were the bones of her. The flesh of her soon to be ash.

There was nothing in the bunny's place but empty grass. I leaned forward into the sink, but I couldn't tell where it had been. Where it had gone. There was nothing there.

This became any other morning.

I made coffee. My husband scrambled eggs. The table set, then cleared.

If the bunny came back, I didn't see it. I meant to wait I did.

Emily Lowe

The Grief Dress

At my mother's funeral, I wore my grief like an old dress, and like an old dress, my grief was ill-fitting. I yanked and clawed to keep it in place.

At my mother's funeral, she wore her death like an expensive dress. I didn't recognize her, all fresh and glossy like she'd fallen asleep at Easter mass. I hadn't seen her this flashy since I was a little girl and she was a new woman, celebrating her first job since my father left with dinner for two at Outback Steakhouse. We both wore our best dresses—ones she'd sewn from McCall's patterns—and she curled our hair.

At my mother's funeral, everyone wore their sadness like rough tulle. It scratched against me with each frown and hug and hand squeeze. My cheeks were raw from their tulle-covered kisses.

At my mother's funeral, my dress of grief was too long and too tight. It tugged at my thighs and puckered against my chest. I'd owned it too many years, through the whole long sickness. My dress of grief made it hard to breathe, hard to walk and bend my elbows. I was so afraid I might tear it and my grief would explode, falling in long black strips to the floor. I imagined the pallbearers slipping on my grief. So, I did not move an inch. I hardly inhaled at all.

At my mother's funeral, the preacher said something long and miserable (his speech was like a dress's train collecting dirt across the floor). I fiddled with my grief's buttons. They were small, punchy painful memories that held my grief together. The time my mother sewed me a prom dress because we couldn't afford the real thing and while she was sewing it, I complained about how cheap the fabric looked. The time I cut up my mother's blouse because I'd been teased for having only two shirts—even though they were both lovely and handsewn with fabric I'd picked myself—and I wanted her to know how I felt; her eyes watered, yet she didn't say a single mean thing. The time I almost got married and my mother climbed into the attic and pulled her old wedding dress from a boxful of mothballs, then held it to the light for me to see. I told her I didn't want any old thing. I told her her marriage had failed.

I never did get married. I never did wear her dress. At my mother's funeral I sat in the front row and wished I'd gone through with the damn thing just to have let my mother's silk line me like a second skin.

At my mother's funeral, my speech was like a sewing machine with no thread. My mouth kept opening and closing, but I couldn't string together any words.

At my mother's funeral, the food was like my mother's wardrobe: all her favorite things brimming with her memory, but what was the point if she wasn't there? There were finger sandwiches and deviled eggs and heaps of strawberry Jell-O, but why have them here if she could not eat them? What was I to do with her hats if they could no longer shade her from the sun?

After my mother's funeral, I could not unbutton my grief. It was much too tight, and I was much too tired. Instead, I lay in bed and stared up at the ceiling. At some point I'd have to alter the grief, open it up, give my body room to breathe in it. But not yet. Even then, I knew I liked how it fit in a way that said *I am here, I am here.* My mother and I had stitched this dress together over her long sickness: every hospital visit, every pill I helped her swallow, every tuft of her lost hair, every hospital bill I tucked away so that she wouldn't see. So many stitches. So much fabric. Enough to wear forever.

Emily Lowe

Smoke

Returning to our farm in New South Wales after the 2019 fires

There are fifty-four of them dead, two hundred sixteen legs in total. Around three thousand kilograms of body, bone, meat, and burnt wool. We pick them up one by one and put them in the back of the truck. They smell of smoke, of roasting, of piss and char, and after we pull them up by their legs and pile them into the heap of the truck bed, so do we. Jack is the one who drives them to the spot where we have dug a mass grave. The bodies fall like bodies. Heavy, without resistance. We shove them out of the truck like bad dreams, letting them layer and fall and fill like a waste dump. *Waste* is what we said when we first saw them. *What a waste.* Waste, the things we don't want, the things we misuse, leave behind, let burn. Some of us think about the irony of it; we bury the burnt bodies because we were not the ones to burn them, because nature licked their tender muscles before we could do the same with an herb rub and a side of Momma's steamed bintje potatoes. Yes, I'm sure some of us think this, but none of us say it. Some of us think instead of the penny lives spilled over the soil. Some of us think of the ghosts of bread and butter and new clothes and new livestock that burned up with them. We talk about these things as we heave the bodies out of the truck, into the ditch. I think of the lamb I helped birth myself—my first, all red and warm and bleating. I named her Maple. She liked to nibble dandelions, but liked blossoms of chicory best.

As the bodies fall, there is the corpse of a lamb. Was it Maple? Or Lemon? Or Charlie Chop? We do not know. The body is black, and besides, no lamb is in that body anyway. The body is all the lambs, but it might as well be none of them, too.

We use the same shovels that made the hole to cover it. We fill in the cracks between teeth and lolling tongues, inside ears, and gashes, and sockets where there are no longer eyes. We fill and fill with dirt and rocks and charred earth until our hole is a soft hill, a fresh memory. We think it also looks like the gentle curve of a womb, but no one says so. It is not a time to look for life in this death.

For the next few weeks, we continue on the scourged earth, plowing up the black clay in search of something that will grow. Instead we find more bits: tongues, a chunk of hoof, a splinted femur.

Daddy does the calling. He tells Uncle Tim in Sydney not to worry. *We still have a couple, yes. No, no more rams. The house is standing. We are standing. We are lucky.*

Ten sheep are still missing. Seven are living, one of them a lamb. We call her Cabbage Patch because that's where we found her once just after she was just born. Her mother is dead or missing. Her brother, Charlie Chop, is dead or missing. Cabbage Patch has burns up her left legs leaving them streaked pink and black. They move up her body as if they are still alive. She can hardly walk without falling.

We keep working and looking and believe less and less that the missing sheep will show. Jack drives the pickup, and we go to our neighbors' farms to help them bury sheep. We go to our neighbor's neighbors' and dig another hole. We move slowly, like a funeral march from farm to farm. We only tire once we are home in bed, clean of soot and sweat, and fall into dreams as black as smoke.

Melissa Goodnight

Margie

I

She's afraid of most animals, dogs especially. Cats, as far as she's concerned, are not hygienic. But I love animals, so on Sunday mornings she grabs a copy of *The Leavenworth Times* and a cup of Diet Coke and takes me to see the bison. It's nothing fancy, just a wire fence around a plot of land on the edge of the U.S. Federal Penitentiary. It's maximum-security, housing the worst offenders my eight-year-old brain can imagine. Murderers, thieves, men who say bad words. But the prison also houses a family of American bison.

In the 1970s it started as two cows and one bull, brought over from Fort Riley, to be housed at the Buffalo Bill Cody Museum. The museum never came to fruition, but the family flourished. Locals flocked to the overlook for picnics; tourists snapped Polaroids. The bison themselves were stoic, still. Their brown eyes reflected faces from the other side of the fence in the heat of the afternoon prairie.

I run along the fence trying to call a calf over. *Not too far!* She shakes her cup into the air as if to threaten me or the animals. I stop short of the last fence post in a row of endless fence posts. There's a brown calf I can almost touch. He looks at me from his patch of grass. I do everything I can to keep his attention. Click my tongue. Try a cartwheel. He's not impressed. I'm about to give up, when he starts over with a loud bellow and I look toward my mother. I thought I wanted to see a seven-hundred-pound calf up close, but suddenly I'm not sure.

He approaches the fence line in a slow gallop, and I walk closer, until only a thin wire separates us. I reach my arm under the break in the fence, and touch his head. His fur lies over his neck and shoulders like a lion, but he has a calm about him that's palpable, even to me. A cow snorts. The calf jumps back, joins her in a gallop toward the herd. *Watch it, Missy!* Ice cup shaking.

II

There were five stairs from the front door of our apartment to the entrance of our building. Inside the living room, my mother snuck her arms around my grandfather and lifted him from his wheelchair. *Careful, sis*, he whispered, motioning to the loose sleeve hanging where an arm should be. I looked away from my mother carrying my ninety-year-old grandfather to the couch, with its muted browns, matching the carpet under my feet.

My sister and I locked eyes; she popped her bubble gum. My mother told her to fold the wheelchair. My sister's slowness prompted my mother's foot tapping while she steadied my grandfather. She watched my sister, grimaced, then stood up quickly and folded it in one swift motion, ignoring my sister's eyes that said she was trying. My mother and sister stood on both sides of the wheelchair, gripped the padded arms, and lifted. I held the door open as they shuffled together, the wheelchair dangling in the space between them.

I raced up the stairs with my sister's glare hot on my neck. At the top, I pushed open the apartment building door, then turned to watch them. I counted their steps. My mother shifted the wheelchair to her good hand. My sister's foot slipped. My mother said to lift higher. My sister hid shame in a smirk.

When they reached the top, I held the door open as they struggled through. They placed the wheelchair into the sunshine, then my mother went back down. My sister stood silent next to me blowing bubbles. I reached up to pop one. She smacked my hand away.

My mother emerged from our basement apartment with my grandfather slung over her shoulder like a sleeping toddler. She grasped the handrail with one arm, while the other held my grandfather. My grandfather, who unbeknownst to me was battling a form of cancer so aggressive that it was attacking his heart, moaned slightly. Unbeknownst to my mother. Unbeknownst to my teenage sister, with her blue eye shadow and her tight white miniskirt, and her hair feathered all the way up to God.

III

I stepped my patent leather shoes into a white square in the checkered linoleum floor, careful to avoid the cracks. I looked up at my mother. She stood silently, staring at the line of people ahead of her. Not smiling, not frowning. I let my body slowly drop toward the square. *No.* That's all my mother had to say, and I was up again, pressing my body into her legs. The papers she held, tucked neatly inside a manila folder, informed the state of Kansas:

> The Child's Birthdate: September 10, 1981
> Mother's Highest Degree of Education: GED
> Father's Name: N/A

My mother's freshly permed hair was neatly sprayed in place. I put my arms around her thick thighs. She stared straight ahead. She smelled of lilacs and sweat. I forced my hand into hers, examining the wrinkles from years of tending tobacco fields, children, and bar. I was hot. We'd walked the four miles to the welfare office. My mother carried me halfway, but it was *my* legs that hurt. I pressed the weight of my body into hers, just about to let my legs buckle, when she looked down at me, then toward a row of green, plastic chairs. Margie surveyed the room, then motioned for me to sit. I raced over to the chairs, ignoring the cracks on the floor.

Darren Demaree

Domestic Mannerism

I hung the apple
& the lemon
from my throat

one obscenely bright morning
to force attention
to the bloom that used to

arrive outside of our house
& each of the children
that caught the new colors

beneath my beard
asked me
about the extreme world

that locked our doors.
I couldn't think to frame
my mouth

around the words
of the garden,
so I sparrow-lipped

the unteaching lessons
of our modern pains
& they let me talk

until they grew hungry
enough to snatch the fruit
with all six hands.

It was pleasant, to be plucked
& still alive. I'll never forget
how their stunted wandering

felt different that day.
They almost traveled
with that skin in their teeth.

Teo Shannon

Her Bedroom

She squirrelled away Tupperware,
stashed food between the bookshelf and wall.
Hid Gladware in the closet under sweaters and laundry.
Our dog bit through her door, chewed the corner-wood free.
There was a maggoty sandwich sandwiched behind the dresser.
We tore it down: tore down the wall, the bed,
ripped the mattress, lit up the dark closet.
Clothes, papers, toys and wrappers and bags.
All manner of debris, putrid, oozing blankets,
pillows of crust, dull crowns of dust.
Puzzle-piece portrait of dolls, frozen in frame,
their porcelain counterparts lining the walls.
Doll after doll, blank glass eyes. One, a nun,
patron of this disaster. Dog hair, sticky notes,
Lip Smacker chapsticks, a broken ballerina music box.
The snapped blinds, the window screen ripped out
A computer riddled with viruses from downloading porn.
An erotic novel she was writing saved on the desktop,
Harlequin Romances hid under the bed.
A whale poster in the closet, the sweater Mom knit
with angora hot-air balloons. Oh, and the smell.
I can't forget the smell. The worst of it all
was the sweet-sick odor of her body spray
trying to cover up the rot. Vanilla. Brown sugar.
I'm ruined for sweet candles and perfumed friends.
When I open leftovers in the fridge, I gag. When I smell
bananas, I have to leave the room. Me, gloved, trash bag in hand.
All of this a portrait of her, her heart, my skin, on display.

Katie Tian

In Which I Write My Father a Birthday Card

I haven't told you this, but I count
myself lucky. At least they spelled your name
right in the obituary. At least the ache
sitting on my chest is a bird's hum now, instead
of a symphony. Every syllable still stings like
cleaving bone from muscle from sinew—but only
sometimes. Others, it runs through me like rivulets
of fountain pen ink, blue & bleeding. I still feel
you, all the time: when I soak plums
in sweet wine, split the lemongrass
stalk-up, play hide-and-seek in
bone-bruising alleyways. Your nectar breath
skittering against my skin when I pour
the tea. I've searched for the remedy
for loss in broken vases and empty
pharmacies and the cracks of my naked
esophagus. I've called the emergency
line twice now in hopes of being saved.
I've rewritten all the photo albums—here are
the pictures of us that I've whittled
down to sawdust. Here is me, swallowing
mouthfuls of sawdust like my mother's
pain. Here is my mother, overflowing
like a melting sun onto kitchen linoleum.
Here is the kitchen that I can't make
a metaphor out of because it is too stained
by the smoldering ghosts of you. There is
no room for grief here, so I've folded

my elegies into another stationary birthday
card that I wear around my throat like
a necklace, or a rope. The shrapnel is pushing
against my teeth. I think this skin
is a time bomb. I think this house
is a mirror. I think I've been
lying though, because the obituary is
in my handwriting. I think I've been lying
because the red of your silhouette looks like
the red of Sunday-night gochujang dinner and
red nectarine syrup and red orchids and
red tongue and beating heart and your red
handprints on my skin and I can't grieve
you, and I can't hate you, because no one
ever taught me the proper way to grieve
something that isn't yet dead.

Kimberly Ann Priest

The Future Is Brighter Than We Think

It's the one thing I did right that I can never remember: bath water not
too hot or cold; the favorite shirt that came out of the wash
for the hundredth time without stains; her birthday cake shaped

like hives surrounded by a dozen sugar cookie bumble bees that she ate
voraciously; the raincoat I gave her printed with tiny cats
and the rain boots that matched and how she wore then all around

the house every day for three weeks straight; popcorn at movies, cotton
candy at carnivals, and the bobblehead flower I found at a tourist
trap on a trip to Arizona that she cupped in her hands as though it were

a whole bouquet; the imperfect pigtails I parted and formed
each morning until a local stylist charged me eighty-five dollars
for bangs, a bob, and pink highlights at her request; the coffee and bagel

outings; the boys I let her talk about for hours while making brownies
then serving her two large portions on a plate embossed with her first
initial; the special milk, the earrings she wore six times

and stashed away, her first and forever tattoo; the way I patiently waited
while she said nothing for days, weeks, months after the divorce;
her nervous fingers gripping a steering wheel and how I told her

she could do this, drive forty-five minutes down a busy highway to come
see me in my new apartment; the car ride during which she confessed
her soul had been saved by a BTS song, "Answer: Love Myself."

Harrison Gatlin

An Education Takes Care

I'm still not convinced I was wrong. See, mortality's a strange thing. And important. It wouldn't have been right if I'd oversimplified it. I know, the eight-year-old brain may not be able to fathom all the depravities of the human soul, fine—Principal McPherson had already belabored this point— but these children of privilege can't hide away in their ivory smocks forever.

That's why I started my third grade private school reading class with "The Lottery" by Shirley Jackson. Where else would you start when trying to unpack the ritual wickedness that's been drilled into the human condition over millennia? Plus, "The Lottery" is canon. Next was The Bible. Oh yes, I went there. Nothing like a nice romp through the fire and brimstone of Revelation to awaken the naked terror of existence that society papers over with its beauty pageants and sports contests. My students reminded me of the apostles, staring dumbly at their leader while the delicious wheels of cogitation turned. I miss them. The way their little minds latched onto the concept of sacrifice was endearing.

"To trade an empty existence for grace and beauty, is that not life's aim?" the children asked.

"Perhaps," I said. "But perhaps it is nothing."

"Was Christ then nothing?" They asked. "Is anything not nothing?"

I have to admit, their interest in nihilism was impressive, albeit dogmatic. I told them just wait until we get to Schopenhauer.

Soon, philistine McPherson caught wind of my free and careful pedagogical mode. He told me I was "overstepping my bounds."

"Bounds!?" I said. "I am a professor of the human soul. Show me its bounds!"

Anyways, I'll have my chance at a discourse with McPherson in a proper court of law before the corpulent madame sings. And I'll be prepared. I was many things as an educator, but a slacker? No, no, no.

We went on to Goya's Black Paintings. Marina Phillips said that she could feel her own mortal heartbeat when she saw Saturn biting the flesh off his son's body. What a thrilling thing to hear as an instructor in the humanities! My students were finally waking up to death! I sensed the hunger in the room, hunger for more than mere theory.

I wanted to intensify our show-and-tell sessions. I considered bringing in a wounded animal—a suffering bird or a raccoon that had barely survived a collision with an SUV—but it wouldn't have worked. Animals' cognitive processes are too simple. You see, we weren't interested in the physical aspect of dying. We sought an understanding of dying qua grappling with the negation of life, and the whole can of psychic worms that opens up.

Luckily, I had a van. Everyone piled in and I improvised a budget-friendly field trip to the Red River Bridge. It was a 333-foot suspension bridge. On the way the kids asked me what's wrong with suicide.

"Nothing's wrong," I said. "It happens."

"We want to try," they said.

"You can't."

"Why not?"

"Because there's no going back."

"So?" they said.

"So you'll be dead."

"What's wrong with being dead?"

"There are moral repercussions. You'll make loved ones suffer."

"But we'll be dead."

"True," I said.

I considered swerving the van and rolling it over the feeble railing of the bridge, killing us all. Perhaps I would meet the gatekeeper and He would thank me for leading so many souls out of their illusory prisons.

But the idea of water rushing into the van and choking each of us as we struggled against the pressure forcing the door shut kept me on the road.

I parked and we waited on the bridge until sunset for a jumper to show. The kids were restless. Their attention spans are shorter than yours or mine. I told them that the majority of jumps occur at night, under the moonlight. I don't know if that's true, but it convinced them. They could be quite gullible. We waited another hour and finally heard sobbing. Our subject was barefoot in a black cocktail dress.

"Why are you doing it?" the kids asked, climbing over one another to glimpse her tears.

"Do you reject the common presupposition that life is real and robust?" they asked. "Are you curious about what awaits you in the vast darkness?"

"My husband's been cheating on me," she said.

"So it's a matter of the total suffering outweighing the total good in your lived experience?" they asked.

"I—I don't know," she sobbed. "I just can't go on."

"We were hoping for a less clichéd answer," they said.

"What?" she said.

"Well, go ahead and do it. We're waiting."

"You want me to … jump? In front of you?"

"What does it matter who watches? You'll be dead."

"I don't want to be watched. Besides, you're children!"

"We're truth-seekers!"

She turned to me: "Are you in charge of these kids?"

"We are masters of our own domains," they said.

"You should be ashamed of yourself," she told me.

"They're masters of their own domains," I said.

Her eyes sought something in mine that she didn't find, and she walked away. The students were outraged.

They screamed at the back of her dress. Then they faced me. "Mr. Langenstein," they said, "teach us more about the ethics of sacrifice." Their goblin fingers wrapped around my legs like small tubers, and they dragged me to the edge of the bridge. They held me against the rail, and Maggie Rogers climbed on my back and pushed my head down, forcing me to contemplate the obsidian surface of the water.

"What do you see?" They asked me.

"Nothing," I said.

"What do you fear?"

"Nothing."

"Lies!"

"You won't do it."

"We'll do it!" they said.

"You won't."

They were probing me for weakness. I hid it. I felt them tugging on my knees, but they couldn't lift me. At last they let go and wandered to the van. The drive back was quiet.

Margaret Emma Brandl

Blue Moon

He says he knows a trick with the orange slice, and then his mouth is somewhere next to hers. They bite the juicy halves as the slice folds in on itself, kissing but for the fact that they're eating the orange, that they're pressing together halves of peel instead of lips. She drops the rind into the glass and slides down next to him on the couch; he stays sitting on the arm—her head against his waist. Overhead, a bright green tube of light is bent into the shape of palm tree leaves, and someone is talking to me but I don't know what they're saying. I hear him say something about mermaids and she moons up at him, heavy-eyed and silly. I recognize the look on her face from the way it felt on mine when I first met him, dazzled by his toothpaste-ad smile and strong jaw and the way he danced like one of those wacky waving inflatable men. He doesn't use social media, doesn't know about the freckled redhead in all of her pictures. They have the same glasses, her boyfriend and him. I excuse myself, slip away unnoticed. It's all colossally unfair.

In the bathroom she's talking to another girl about how confusing and lovely it is to be around him, how she still isn't *sure*. I wait in the stall, pretending poorly that I'm not listening; they linger at the sink and I smile insincerely as I wash my hands. Our orientation team is supposed to work well together. On Monday we'll be back in the student center, going in twenty different directions as once, counting with a clicker how many people are in the auditorium and repeating for the millionth time how to get to the library and texting each other when we come across someone with a weird name. We'll be impressive and professional, operate like a well-oiled machine. If this were late July—if this were the last session of freshman orientation—I'd say something now. But the fact is it's mid June and I need the money and she's best friends with the grad assistant who works for our boss. I hold my tongue and the door.

I follow them back to the corner we've claimed as our own, and all I can do is watch as he follows where she goes, how she leans her head close to speak to him and he mirrors her. There is low light and a bit of a quiet buzz in my brain, a sleepiness I should welcome, and everyone is drinking Blue Moon. Something burns in my chest when he excuses himself to walk her out, the green neon over our heads reflecting in his glasses. I can't read his expression when he walks back in, just a few minutes later, minutes like hours, and turns to talk to someone else.

When we all leave—the rest of us—and stumble back toward campus, I look up into the sky as if it's there to give me answers. I imagine that I am the heroine of the story, that I'm the girl who orange-peel-kissed a boy who most definitely wants her the way she might want him. He's somewhere up ahead with someone else, doesn't notice as I hang back. I'd think the moon would be out in full force on a night like this, but it's just a sliver, a fingernail, a slim chance getting slimmer.

She asks me about it later, about the orange, as if it's a secret, as if she's worried there are pictures. I don't try to be nice. *Everyone saw*, I tell her, but maybe I just mean I did.

Jamie Odeneal

Cash Grab

Leave it to Jared to throw a damper on her fun.

Her husband sat on the bed to remove his loafers. The left shoe took the black sock off with it, revealing a pasty white foot with a patch of dark hair.

"It's embarrassing, Cher," Jared said, rescuing the sock and tugging it back on. "Scrambling around on the floor, snatching at dollar bills like that, in front of everybody."

"On the *ice*," Cheryl corrected, because the distinction mattered. Floors were places people shuffled around, carrying in filth from the street. Ice was sparkling and clean, or at least she hoped it would be. By the time the contest started, the rink could be fairly scuffed already. There could even be blood. She remembered the last Chipmunks game they'd attended, how there'd been a scuffle at the far end of the rink. Cheryl didn't see how it began, but it ended in a churning mass of helmets, sticks, and skates, players clutching onto each other's jerseys, leaving just enough distance to land punches. Cheryl had found the skirmish much more exciting than the actual game, which they only attended because Jared had gotten free tickets at work. How thrilled she'd felt when one of the players pulled off his helmet, revealing a face like wet, raw meat, and spat a crimson chunk onto the ice.

Cheryl couldn't remember now if they Zamboni'd after that or if she'd only imagined the brushes of the beast sweeping up the tooth and its trickle of gore, leaving a pristine stripe of ice in its wake.

"It's the division finals," Jared continued. "Everyone we know will be there. The Pattersons, the Kaczmareks, the people from the bank, obviously."

Cheryl suspected that was his real hang-up. First National Bank was sponsoring the event, donating five thousand dollars in one-dollar bills "for our county's hardworking and underappreciated teachers." Cheryl did feel underappreciated, and she wondered why her husband didn't feel the same. Jared had been at the same small branch of Fox Hunt Bank, a much smaller operation than First National, for eighteen years now. He'd interviewed for three different management jobs at First National but had yet to snag a position, not even a lateral move. As he shrugged off each rejection, she wondered why it didn't bother him more. Where was the Jared she'd dated years ago, the one she used to watch playing basketball? He'd been scrappy then, tall and lean, sexy-slick with sweat, quick to throw an elbow or sweep a foot, whatever it took to keep the ball.

These days, during the odd pickleball sessions with Bill and Tammy Kaczmarek, Jared was easily winded and couldn't be bothered to keep an accurate score count. Cheryl always knew the score, especially when playing against their oldest and dearest friends. Off the court, it seemed the Kaczmareks were winning at everything these day since Bill had parlayed an inheritance into a chain of rolled ice-cream shops. Cheryl didn't understand the appeal of watching some teenager spend ten minutes scraping together your cookies and cream, but the venture had proved lucrative. Bill and Janet, formerly an insurance salesman and a preschool receptionist respectively, now boasted a new Tesla, a St. Thomas timeshare, and season tickets for the Chipmunks. They could stand to lose a few pickleball games.

Cheryl knew a big reason for Jared's career plateau was that he didn't present well enough for a place like First National. His hair was buzzed in a way that read more "wrestling coach" than "financial manager," and his baggy suits and worn loafers were the very picture of middle-management mediocrity. Whenever she'd encourage him to take advantage of the BOGO sale on suits at Jos. A. Banks, he'd tell her, "This isn't Wall Street, Cher. When it comes to money, the people here trust people who look like them. Anyway, we have more important things to spend our money on."

Jared had a point. Their daughter Rosie would be off to college in less than two years. Since a devastating breakup with an underwhelming shit named Brayden, Rosie was hell-bent on heading west after graduation. And the house, only ten years old when they'd bought it as newlyweds, now needed a new roof. Cheryl tried to care about the roof, but the living room carpet seemed more pressing. No matter how tidy she kept the house, her eyes constantly drifted to the bleached-out spots where Muffin liked to take a piss.

She knew she shouldn't keep score, but expenses like roofs and carpets were generally covered by her labor and not Jared's, whose salary and hours were fixed. Cheryl was the one who'd taken on an extra section of AP Lit for the past few years, who'd spent her Saturdays tutoring the intellectually incurious children of better-off families. And what did she get for her efforts? Each time they put aside a little extra, another non-negotiable expense would rear its head. Like when they added a third driver to the family insurance policy. Or when the vet recommended a three-hundred-dollar senior blood panel for Muffin. Of course there were negotiable expenses, too, like when her husband replaced their old but serviceable grill with a Weber like Bill's. (She'd let him have that one; it was frankly a turn-on to see his competitive streak reemerge.)

The next big expense, according to Jared, had to be a new roof, though Cheryl didn't understand the point of replacing something nobody would even notice. When she told Jared about putting her Cash Grab winnings towards new carpet, he brought up something about finding "shingle granules in the downspout." But his main objection to the event was that everybody would see her, which only sweetened the deal for Cheryl.

She already had her outfit planned: a white, fuzzy V-neck sweater and a pair of stretchy, black jeans she'd ordered off Amazon. With rips at the knees, the jeans were impractical for crawling on ice, but the contest wouldn't last more than a few minutes anyway. She wanted to look sexy for once, not just in old throwback pictures on Facebook, but in real life. Cheryl could already feel the sharp, cool air of the arena, the crisp bills crinkling in her hands as she bent over to take what was hers. Let them look at her ass if they wanted. The Kaczmareks, the Pattersons, her coworkers, they would all see her, admire her fashion sense, her youthful figure, and her willingness to embrace a good time.

"No way in hell I'm going," Rosie had said the night before the game as she sat on the sofa tapping through Snapchats.

Cheryl had just retrieved the complimentary tickets from the printer and was hoping to firm up their plans for the next evening. She'd give Rosie a pass, she decided. The girl already suffered enough from having her mother teach at her school; she was loath to jeopardize Rosie's social capital any further. Jared, however, had no excuse.

"You're coming, right?" she asked her husband.

"I don't know, Cher," he said as he scraped his spoon against the bottom of his ice cream bowl. Muffin hovered nearby, waiting to lick the remnants.

"I'm going by myself?"

Participating in something outrageous like this was only acceptable with her husband's support. He needed to walk her in, cheer her on, celebrate with her afterwards. Without Jared as her wingman, she risked looking rather pathetic in front of the Pattersons, the Kaczmareks, and her coworkers.

"Now I don't want to go at all!" she said, though of course she'd still go. She'd already narrowed her carpet options down to Oat Straw or Seashore Fog.

"It's just not my kind of thing," Jared said.

"And that fantasy football draft was my kind of thing?"

"I thought you had a good time."

"Making conversation with those boring wives over Crock-Pot meatballs, I did that for you! I didn't even complain about it."

"I remember you complaining," Rosie added.

"I'm sure someone will take a video," Jared said, lowering the ice-cream bowl to the floor so Muffin could have her share.

The next evening, Cheryl was still angry as she primped in their overheated bathroom. She sipped on a hefty pour of pinot grigio to settle her nerves, but it failed to calm her. As she struggled with her hair, she was sweating through her makeup base, and the tag in her sweater was chafing the back of her neck. She took another sip of her wine, which had lost its chill and now tasted as cheap as it was.

Jared's complaint, that "everyone we know will be there," had started to feel like a threat.

"Lookin' good, Cher!" Jared called from the bed. She suspected the compliment was a peace offering, but unless he'd changed his tune about coming, she refused to shift into détente.

Cheryl was attempting her last section of beachy waves when, just over the line of boozy, she burned her wrist with her curling iron.

"Shit!" she hissed.

A few seconds later, Jared appeared behind her in the mirror. His eyes moved from her wrist to the wineglass.

"Want me to drive you?" he asked.

She made him wait for her answer as she sprayed her curls with a fresh layer of TRESemmé.

"Fine," she finally said as the mist settled.

Later, as Jared pulled his Subaru onto the main road, they passed a trio of chain restaurants: Hardee's, Sonic, and Applebee's, which Cheryl always thought of as: Jared's choice, Rosie's choice, and her choice. It never made sense why anyone would choose fast food in front of the TV over getting dressed up and having someone serve you a nice meal.

She was still furious Jared wasn't coming, but she was also hurt that he didn't care enough to stop her. If he thought the contest was so embarrassing, shouldn't he put his foot down? There was a time when he would have fought with her over something like this. Like at her cousin Heather's wedding years ago, when somebody's plus-one got handsy with her on the dance floor. "You totally embarrassed me!" Jared fumed on the entire drive home. "That guy *knew* we were together, and you let him grind all over you!" It didn't matter that Cheryl had found the young man harmless or that Jared refused to dance with her. He wouldn't stop ranting about it until later that night when she reassured him with a blow job that he was her one and only.

He drove in silence now, shoulders hunched around his ears.

She flipped down the mirror.

"Can you close that, Cher? The light makes it hard to see."

She took her time swiping on a layer of lip gloss before snapping the visor back up. They rode the rest of the way in silence.

When Jared pulled up to the arena entrance, he said only, "Text when you're ready to leave."

Cheryl made a big show of separating her ticket from his and leaving it behind on the seat.

Once inside, Cheryl scanned for familiar faces as she hustled to the designated meeting area. If she searched hard enough, she was sure to find coworkers and friends, but it was just as well nobody saw her arriving alone.

She hustled to the roped off section for contest participants, where she spotted members of the WJMA crew in matching fleece vests, along with Suzanne Maclaren, a brassy-haired local anchor who'd been on air longer than Cheryl had been alive. The other participants, she noted, were decked out in gear from their school, sweatshirts and beanies in their team colors. She tugged at her fluffy white sweater, which was itchier than it looked and clingy around her midsection. Instead of socializing with her competition, she parked herself on a folding chair and scrolled through makeup tutorials on TikTok.

By the end of the first period, she was all jangled nerves and pent-up resentment at Jared. Still, when the organizer announced, "It's showtime!" Cheryl was ready to compete. She pushed to the front of the line, squared her shoulders, and stepped onto the ice.

The Cash Grab, which she'd been anticipating for weeks, was over in a flash.

Much later, when she watched the video of the contest, Cheryl saw something very different than the strangers online who criticized her. Or not her, exactly, but the event itself. Where she saw a group of spunky educators engaged in rowdy competition, others saw only debasement and humiliation.

She was shocked that the event had landed in the public sphere the way it had. Within days, the clip began circulating nationally. The social media mob ramped up its outrage, and it seemed nobody found the event either fun or inspiring. Even her principal, who had planned to show the video on the morning announcements, had soured on it.

"Probably best to let the hubbub die out on its own," Dr. Molina told her. "But congrats on your winnings!"

In watching the video, it seemed clear to Cheryl that she was the one to beat from the beginning. While the other teachers were clowning around, mugging to the crowd, Cheryl stood at the front of the pack, still and focused with her knees bent and eyes trained on the two bank employees dumping the contents of the garbage bag onto the center circle.

She remembered feeling spring-loaded, fueled by nerves, and ready to launch. She scanned the crowd, hoping to feel encouraged by the sight of a familiar face. For a split second, she thought she'd spotted Tammy Kaczmarek's chunky highlights, but before she could confirm, she heard the buzzer.

Cheryl threw herself down onto the ice, anchored her knees, and began raking the cash inwards and down into the V of her sweater.

The crowd, the crisp air, the competition, even her anger at Jared, all disappeared as she got to work. Once in motion, she transformed into a cross between a Hungry Hungry Hippo and a money-sweeping Zamboni. She was peripherally aware of bodies knocking into her on either side, but she kept her eyes on the clusters of bills. An especially large body careened in from the side, and Cheryl landed hard on her left shoulder, then sprang right back up, feeling no pain at all. She continued grabbing, grabbing, now double-time, using her hips and elbows to body-check anyone else who got too close.

By the time the final buzzer sounded, she was drenched with sweat and her fists and white sweater were stuffed with bills. It was only when she watched the video later that she noticed her how her exaggerated girth made her resemble a snowman.

She'd felt nothing but adrenaline at the time, but the video showed a woman who had given herself over to the effort. In just sixty seconds, her hair had turned stringy and mascara ran down her cheeks, scarlet from the exertion. But even redder were her knees, which were scraped and bleeding down into the rips of her jeans. Her chest heaved as she stood clutching two giant wads of cash. A single bill floated out of her cleavage and onto the ice.

"A little aggressive, don't you think?" sneered the woman next to her, cradling her own smaller pile of bills.

Cheryl was about to respond when the music started back up and the crowd cheered the teachers' retreat from the ice.

It wasn't until after the representatives from First National had converted her winnings to a check that she took stock of her injuries. She accepted gauze and bandages from a medic and shivered as she tended to her own wounds. The skin on both knees was shredded, her hips ached, and her left shoulder throbbed beneath the disposable ice pack. She could hear the crowd roaring as the Chipmunks returned to the ice.

Once she'd bandaged her knees and stashed her check, Cheryl texted Jared: *Meet you out front.*

She had almost hobbled all the way to the exit when she spotted Tammy and Bill Kaczmarek. Aware of how wretched she looked, she tried to change course behind a group of rowdy twenty-somethings. Too late. Tammy waggled her fingers from across the crowd.

"Oh, my, look at you!" Tammy said as she and Bill approached.

"So much fun, right?" Cheryl said as she struggled to zip her coat while holding both her purse and swag bag from the bank.

"You really went for it," Tammy said, dropping her eyes to Cheryl's bandaged knees. Tammy Kaczmarek née Stefano, her oldest friend, would never have to scrounge on an ice rink for new living room carpet, and that stung more than her injuries.

"Where's Jared?" Bill asked, flashing his newly capped white teeth.

"He just went to get the car." She squinted through the windows to see if she could spot Jared's car, but between the bright lights inside and darkness outside, it was impossible to see anything.

"You guys aren't staying for the whole game?" Bill said. "It's the finals!"

"Honey, look at her. I'm sure she wants to get home and clean up." Tammy chuckled and added, "My, my, what they put teachers through these days."

As if Tammy hadn't spent the better part of the last decade answering phones at Our Lady of Sorrows Preschool. Under the fluorescent lights, she noticed Tammy's teeth looked even whiter than Bill's. Almost blue.

"Tell Jared we're sorry we missed him," Bill said.

Tammy opened her enormous Coach purse then and started digging, "Let me find those gift cards I've been meaning to give you. You really need to stop by the new store in Springhouse Common. Just opened last week!"

"I'm not big on ice cream."

"A treat for Rosie and Jared, then." Tammy pressed a slim stack of gift cards into Cheryl's hand. "On us."

"Speak of the devil!" said Bill.

Cheryl turned to see her husband pushing his way through the crowd. She was at once furious that he hadn't come earlier when it had mattered and grateful that he was here now, when it might have mattered more.

Cheryl swung the First National bag around to cover her knees. Jared was bound to make a fuss about her injuries later, to carp on why she put herself through all this just to win a little money. If he were just going to scold her, she preferred it to happen at home, not in front of their friends.

When he reached their group, Jared leaned down and planted a kiss on Cheryl's cheek, then hooked an arm around her waist.

"You were an animal out there, Cher!" He turned to grin at the Kaczmareks. "Did you guys see her?"

Cheryl felt his arm tighten and wondered if he'd really been out there cheering her on, but she would never ask in front of Bill and Tammy.

"Cheryl always was quite the competitor," Tammy said.

"Damn straight! Beast mode, am I right?" Jared said, pumping a fist. "You guys take care. I'm gonna get my girl home."

As they headed towards the exit, Cheryl hoped the Kaczmareks got a good look at her ass, which was still better than Tammy's after all these years.

"You came?" she asked once they were outside.

"Rosie called and yelled at me, told me get in there."

"Actually called, not texted?"

"I know, I thought the house was on fire or something."

"You came because of Rosie."

Jared stopped and reached over to tuck a straggly strand of hair behind Cheryl's ear.

"She was right, though," he said. "I couldn't let you do it alone."

But Cheryl had done it alone, or had felt alone, anyway. Her husband was here now, though, and he'd been there for her run-in with the Kaczmareks. That would have to be enough because Cheryl didn't have the strength to carry her grudge further into the night.

He pointed to the canvas bag in her hand. "Got some free stuff?"

Cheryl hadn't examined the contents yet, but she guessed it was typical swag, beer koozies and lanyards and such, all of it bearing the logo of a bank that wouldn't hire her husband. At least not yet. There was bound to be another BOGO sale on suits soon, and next time, she wouldn't take no for an answer.

Nearly three weeks had passed since the event, and Cheryl's scraped knees and curling iron burn were healing, though the Internet shame still lingered. She spent more time than she'd care to admit scrolling through the Twitter comments on WJMA's original post, as well the responses to First National's apology.

A sad commentary on the way this nation treats its teachers!
The opposite of heartwarming—completely dehumanizing
Just give them the money instead of humiliating them!

The comments on her original Facebook post had been largely supportive, but in the wake of the outrage, she ultimately deleted it.

At least nobody could take away her winnings, which were more than double what everybody else had grabbed and enough to replace the living room carpet. She'd settled on a mid-grade pile density with a high-grade padding, a speckled beige made with SmartStrand technology to repel stains. Installation was scheduled for Saturday.

Thursday afternoon, Cheryl came home to find Muffin whining at the slider and Rosie on the sofa staring at her phone.

"Rosie! Don't you hear this dog begging to go out?"

Her daughter plucked an AirPod from her ear. "She won't stay out in the rain."

Cheryl opened the slider and pushed the elderly cockapoo out with her stocking foot. Next, she headed into the kitchen to unpack her lunch tote.

And stepped directly into a puddle.

"For christ's sake," Cheryl muttered. "You gotta make sure she goes!" she called toward the living room.

Ignoring her wet feet for now, she grabbed the roll of paper towels and squatted to mop up the mess. She had just pressed the wad into the puddle when she felt a cold drop land on the back of her neck. She looked up to find the source and was hit with another drop, this one right in the middle of her forehead.

Cheryl got up off her knees, still tender from the contest, and fetched a pasta pot from the cabinet. She positioned it under the leak.

Sometimes you had to make do with what you had.

Cheryl understood there were moments when you got your shot on the ice, when you elbowed out the competition and grabbed what you could. Sometimes that competition might even be your best friend since childhood, and what you grabbed was the guy with the nicest eyes, the taller of the two standing at the bar, the one with the good job at the bank, waiting to buy you both drinks. You and this taller one start planning your future together because he makes it clear from the get-go that he's all in. A mortgage and a baby later, you realize he's not quite the trophy you thought he was, and sure, your ambition has surpassed his, but at least he's loyal.

You learn to be satisfied with this man, this stalled-out bank manager in the nubby fleece and bad loafers, because he will show up for you when it counts, eventually. He will even run you a hot bath when you're sore and weary, will tend to your injuries, dab your knees with Neosporin, kiss your bruises, kiss you wherever you like. Because he knows you are a prize fighter.

You learn to live with what you have, what you have fought for, your prize being steadfastness in the end.

Later that evening, as Jared snoozed in his chair, Cheryl sipped her second glass of wine and browsed Overstock.com for a rug to cover the piss stains, something stylish but practical, not too expensive. It would have to do.

Abigail Chang

Fishbowl

Fishbowl hates himself. Fishbowl is glass. Fishbowl could fit in a bottle. There's glassware clogging his drains—he's all huddled at the bottom. Wisps of cloud. Maybe wave. Fishbowl tries to make waving motions with his arms. There's lead shot through his fins. Just heft. Maybe noose. Catch this: Fishbowl moves into another Fishbowl; his old one was too small. Thirty days crept up too quick and suddenly the walls were closing in on him. The landlord shot up his door. Go faster. Wipe up behind you. We'll be your caretaker. All of Fishbowl's things could fit in a box: plastic beads, water lily, mango husk. Rattle. Disks fall out of his stomach, CDs and love letters squatting on the tile. Weave. You're running out of time. Are we there yet? Ring the doorbell. Your mother doesn't care for you. She's in a purple bathrobe, holding open the door, telling you go go go go go. Faster. I'm about to collapse behind you. So Fishbowl cradles the box in his hands and runs. Out the backyard, through the fence, he scales a tree. God it's so high up. He can see the world rupturing, gash tearing across Manhattan, rivers oozing this thick, bloody syrup. There's goop everywhere. Lust in the air. It was all your fault. Why didn't you? Could you have ever? Whatever, it doesn't matter, you were too slow. As the world settles around him, Fishbowl takes his head off, holds it in his hands like it could shatter any moment. He's nothing without his head and he knows it. When he feels the air swoop through him—this thin beam of blue cracking, edging through the glass—he weeps, he weeps hard. He bites at his own thumb. This terrible animal sound rips out from his lips. If he strains his ears, he can just make out this noise coming from the house: Somebody is scrubbing the pipes, going at them hard, making a great racket.

Daniel Zeiders

Woolaroc

Around the corner from the snack bar
     hiding in its own little stable
     with walls painted green and gold tallgrass prairie
         there is an old buffalo
           wooly and brown
           with patches of fur worn off
           dead and stuffed

Fed on a diet of receipts napkins wrappers
A vacuum inside sucks the garbage out of visitor's hands
     brave kids place their palms to its mouth
         to feel the suction and hear the squeal of pressure
     mean kids feed it pennies that clatter into its belly

At night
     drunk on coins and trash
     it climbs over its pen and roams
         between statues and buildings
         with its electric cord dragging behind

It studies the murals of cordless buffalo
     how they nuzzle their calves
     hovering their noses over the grass
         pulling the field into their mouths
           while hunters wait above

It lumbers over to the field of grass
     a belly of jangling change

And even though the vacuum is powerless
      it lowers its head to the ground
           and tries to suction up the thick blades of grass

In brief sparks
      the motion of it brings back
           the feeling that it used to love this
                filling itself from the land
But it can't remember what grass tasted like
      It pretends
           maybe

                like a napkin
                    smeared with ketchup

Daniel Zeiders

Water Towers

A high school prank way back when
Hot   Warm   Cold
painted on the three water towers
because she hated this town enough to
ladder up each one in the night
and maybe make her friends laugh
bust the knuckles of pearl-clutchers
wringing their hands at the graffiti

The next morning the work is proclaimed
Cool   Quirky   Artistic
the newspaper reports "just what this
humble town needed" and a man is paid
to come and re-do the paint bigger and
bolder and spotlights planted at the base
light the words at night and people from
all over come look and take pictures

Jesus Christ is there nothing worse than
State   Sanctioned   Vandalism
and now when she comes home to visit
she drives by and her boyfriend points
to the time her little rebellion was whole-
heartedly devoured and ingested by the
town and laughing asks her if that isn't
just the stupidest thing she has ever seen

Ellen June Wright

Portrait of the Subject as a Free Bird

after Aaron F. Henderson

Here's what it means to be Black in a man's body—images not in
chains, not bullet riddled. Zoot-suited James "Jump Sharp" Johnson
or weekend-casual fathers and sons. They wear Tims sometimes.
Ordinary men at the center of the canvas, hanging on the wall (not
a tree) the way Napoleon's portrait hangs in Europe's galleries. One
smiles like Jesus after a miracle, dreadlocks flowing down his back;
another ages gracefully, hair like pepper sprinkled on snow. Their
piercing gazes search me from the canvas. "KL the Bass Man" sounds
a blues guitar. Like "Watchmen on the Walls of Zion," "Deacons"
hold shotguns and pistols against false worshippers, invaders of the
bible study or shots fired in the night. They look so familiar, I want
to call them brothers, father, friends. These men freeing themselves
of fetters are ancestors, laborers almost done toiling, educators.
Blackness does not hang heavy on them; they wear it like moonlight.

Matt Rowan

Entirely Skull

He'd had the procedure but suddenly felt a little silly about it, after the fact. Even though it was irreversible, even though he was irreversibly his new self.

He turned to the TV. The man on the TV had explained the procedure in a way he'd understood.

The man on TV spoke hurriedly, like he was trying to hurry past what he was saying so he could just reap the benefits, "Welcome to the I Am Entirely Skull commercial, folks. Why have a body? Why not just have a skull and roll around? Why, you ask? I got to thinking, where do I feel entirely safe? Inside my own head! The answer was obvious. Entirely skull, *be* entirely skull."

That was why the man on the television was now only a free-standing, much-larger-than-normal-sized skull. He'd revolutionized a procedure that allowed him to live in his own head, sort of. His brain was installed in there, and some other parts—the most essential parts. Which ones are "essential"? "Oh, just the ones you cannot imagine yourself living without," the man on the TV said. "Though they do little actual use now, for me it's my arms. You can't see them, of course, but I'm wiggling them with gusto." The man on the TV rolled a bit back and forth to help the viewers visualize his arms moving within his new, overlarge skull.

The man on the TV, who was just a skull, stood to speak, or standing was clearly the image meant to be conveyed, but the truth was, given his being a skull, there really was no true means of standing anymore. So he, the man on TV, as entirely skull, positioned himself in a way reflecting both what comes to mind when a person is sitting or standing, perpetually caught between or enmeshed in both the world of the standing and the sitting. It was, really, a leaning upward on his jawbone and then, as it proved impossible to maintain his balance, the man on TV, as skull, rolled over on his side.

The commercial ended abruptly.

He breathed a sigh of relief.

The man on the TV hadn't lied to him. He was, indeed, happier this way. Nothing but a skull was needed to get along just fine in an otherwise complicated and unsettling world. "Stay inside it and never look out," he said to himself as he rolled out his front door.

He looked around outside, taking notice of a few birds who appeared untrustworthy. "Eagles that speak and keep track of my thoughts," he said to himself, as he began to roll down the especially vertiginous sidewalk near his home, feeling fragile like an egg, and, oh no, descending ever more rapidly as he found himself completely incapable of stopping.

Bryan D. Price

Herculaneum #13

How many Easters has it been since he washed her feet? It became an April ritual for him. Now he could only sit down to compose a few lines about her fealty to resurrection narratives. She gave him her tongue and he kept it very safe, took exceedingly good care of it. There's not an organ alive, he thought, better fit for crossing the boundary between platonic and erotic love. He had great affection for that tongue and all that it could do. The sounds that it made, like being awakened by a lightning storm or the birth of a completely new language entering his consciousness as fully formed as a moth or a butterfly.

Blake Johnson

Play It Again, Petey

For reasons I still don't understand, Jess—my first and last serious girlfriend—was intent on marrying me. But before this could happen, I had to be submerged beneath a river filled with sludge and cast-off debris in the name of her faith. We were both seventeen.

I went to check out the river beforehand with Petey, my best friend at the time, in hopes he'd talk me out of the whole thing. But he was more interested in puffing on a blunt and taking video with an ancient, cumbersome camcorder he'd stolen from a yard sale. The camera was so big he had to rest it on his shoulder to keep it level. The blunt was dwindling down to its last embers.

There was no beauty in that dismal autumn, and even less at the river. The slate-gray waters seemed to bubble as if laced with chemicals. The smell of oil and damp plastic steamed off its tainted surface. Honestly, it was little more than a thoroughfare through which pollution found its way to the vast ocean, where it could be safely forgotten.

I sat down on the craggy beach. Petey stood a few feet behind me and spun in place, both arms wrapped around the camera as if it were the only thing tethering him to the earth. Eventually he quit spinning, tottered on past me, and spat his dead blunt into the river. I winced, half expecting the water to catch on fire. But it just drifted along the current, farther and farther, until it wasn't even worth thinking about anymore.

He squatted. Hefted up a rock with his free hand.

"You should throw this at me," Petey said.

"Are you serious?"

"Hell, yeah." He held the rock in front of the lens. "It'll look like a meteor crashing."

I chewed the inside of my cheek. I sat on my hands. Petey dropped the rock.

What can be said about Petey? He always wore a battered brown fishing hat and had never been fishing. His dimples were so pronounced they seemed swollen. He often asked me to do shameful and embarrassing things, and I usually did them. I loved him. I loved him because he never asked me to be anything other than what I was.

He stepped closer to the water's edge, stared into its bleak surface. My eyes followed his gaze—a wave of dizziness crashed over me.

"I bet people have drowned here," Petey said.

I tried to think of a retort, a comeback, even a rebuke. But I couldn't. I'd been having the exact same thought myself.

Petey hefted the camera from one shoulder to the other. "They should just use a fucking pool."

"The water needs to be natural or something."

"Why?"

"Jess said so."

At the name *Jess*, Petey snorted. He whirled around, turned the camera on me, and finally addressed the issue at hand.

"So you're really going through with it?"

This is what I'd been waiting for. My vocal cords quivered with an urgent message: Jess was my only chance. Something deeper than instinct had given me a glimpse at all my potential futures—if I did not go through with the baptism, my life would spin off in some wild direction beyond my control where I would probably die before the then-unimaginable age of thirty. Once I bloomed into who I was destined to become, no one like Jess would ever accept me, and it was people like Jess who ordered the world.

I had hoped to tell him this. But he was recording my every movement, my every word, and I couldn't bear for the truth to be documented like that. I knew he wouldn't stop even if I asked because that would break the rules of the game he was playing, and games were the only thing he cared about.

"I guess," was all I said.

"But you're a shitty swimmer."

Which was true. My body always felt heavy as soon as it touched water. I tried to explain this to Jess, but she had just pursed her lips and folded her arms. I knew then that she would never sympathize with my cowardice.

Petey stood there, holding the camera steady. He made a twirling motion with his fingers. I sighed and picked up a rock.

"Go stand over there," I said.

Petey grinned. His red dimples gleamed like boils. He lit up another blunt, then took his position to document the apocalypse.

The baptism didn't happen right away. I still hadn't taken the class at Jess's church. So she picked me up outside my house on a Sunday afternoon, because I didn't have a car and she did. She had started saving for it before she even had a learner's permit. It was a deep blue SUV that perpetually glimmered and always had a full tank. She kept telling me I could buy one, too, if I worked hard and made a plan, but I didn't believe that. I never would.

She pulled up, and I slid into the passenger's seat; she smirked and leaned over to kiss me. Then the rear door opened and Petey got in, camera slung over his shoulder. Jess froze. I stared at my filthy sneakers, tracking dirt on the upholstery.

"Petey stayed over last night," I said. "Figured he could tag along."

I snuck a glance at Jess. She was smiling now, but it was a thin and quivering smile.

"Are you sure you want to come, Pete?" she said. "It's going to be boring."

He had already started filming, camera aimed at Jess. He said nothing, only made the twirling motion with his fingers, as if urging us to drive on. Jess raised her eyebrows. Mouthed something to me. I knew exactly what she was asking. I stared out the window and pretended not to see.

We made our way to Jess's church. Petey stuck the camera out the window, recording the scroll of small, beaten houses and overgrown lawns that made up my neighborhood. Then, a few turns later, we were thrust into downtown, surrounded by tall brick buildings and monochrome streets. I wondered if Petey had managed to capture the point where one morphed into the other.

"People did drown there," Petey said as the church came into view. "A few kids. I looked it up."

I kept my mouth shut. I turned away so he couldn't record me envisioning watery graves and interminable depths.

Movement, next to me. Jess's fingers interlaced with my own. I glanced sidelong at her, and my heartrate steadied. I let myself sink into my seat. I don't think I loved her, not in the way she deserved to be loved, but I believed in her. God, did I believe in her.

The pastor's office was bright, so bright I had to squint at everything. The floor put me in mind of a thin sheet of ice. Jess and I sat down with the other participants—a young woman with eyebrow piercings and an older man gripping his knees—on cream-colored couches sheathed in plastic. Petey was outside somewhere. As soon as we pulled into the parking lot, he disappeared behind the building, mumbling something about a smoke.

The pastor sat in a plush chair, hands steepled, leaning forward. He wore a shirt that molded itself to lean muscle. His lats flared like mutated wings. He reminded me of a Roman deity, the kind of pagan god you could be damned just for knowing. He kept on nodding, as if he had said something profound, even though no one had said a word yet.

I still wasn't entirely sure what Jess believed. Her religion involved long periods of silence interspersed with spontaneous shouts. There were lots of pictures of Jesus in the church, but I don't think he had much to do with anything. I had hoped the class would make sense of things, that it would quiet my trembling hands and reveal a brighter future than the one hurtling toward me.

But the pastor's words didn't help. It was all about dying then coming back changed, becoming someone else, and it was supposed to be symbolic, a mere simulated death, but I couldn't help but think how transformation did not invalidate demise, how who I was now would pass away. I wanted to take Jess's hand, but her hands were folded in prayer; I wasn't strong enough to pull them apart.

The pastor stressed that this was a commitment. He went around the room, asking us one by one if we were ready. The woman with the eyebrow piercing said yes and gave the room a double thumbs-up. The older man nodded his head like a piston. All eyes fell on me.

"Well, son?" the pastor said.

Silence. I felt Jess watching me, the heat of her gaze boring holes in my skull. She's seeing it all, I thought. She's staring right into my brain. The pastor massaged his chin, as if I were some deep mystery that could be solved given enough contemplation. I tried to force out the word yes. I opened my mouth and clamped it back shut, then opened it again.

The door burst open. The stink of smoke and skunk grass flooded the office. Petey stood in the threshold, wielding the camcorder. The interruption was so absurd, so sudden, that we were all caught in an inescapable stasis. Even the pastor was too stunned to speak. Petey turned in a slow, horizontal arc, capturing each wide-eyed expression. When the lens fell on me, Petey put two fingers to his lips.

"Shh," he said. "I'm a hidden camera."

Jess sprung up from the couch and jabbed her thumb at the exit, over and over again, like she was trying to spear something to death. And Petey bobbed his head in response and trained the lens on Jess, either completely misunderstanding her sharp gesture or understanding it completely and not caring. I let out a slow breath that I hoped sounded exasperated.

"I'm sorry," I said, standing up and shepherding Petey away. "I'm really sorry."

The pastor didn't say anything, just sat there with his mouth hanging open. I pushed Petey out of the room and felt every muscle in my body unclench.

The drive back was quiet, save for Jess flinging laughable insults at Petey every so often—things like *You're a real piece of work* and *I hope you're pleased with yourself*, phrases that belonged amidst the pantheon of television cliches, not on the lips of a girl who had yet to live the bulk of her life. I spent the whole ride cradling my face in my hands, trying not to let any giggles or tears slip between my fingers.

Petey responded by patting the camera. He said, "I can't wait to watch this."

We dropped him off and returned to my house. We idled in the driveway and tried to figure out how to talk to each other. There was something separating us in that moment, like an electric field. It hummed and sparked with all our differences.

She spoke. The tone of her voice was years removed from her place in time.

"He's your best friend. I know that."

"Yeah."

"But I don't know if you have the strength to keep him in your life."

I blinked. "The strength?"

"He'll drag you down."

"It's just the way he is."

She shifted in her seat. She reached across the space between us and ran her hand through my hair.

"It's not who you have to be," she said. "Will you be there next week?"

I paused a second too long. She shook her head and unclicked the locks. My heart slammed against my chest as I imagined her receding from my life forever.

"I'm not a strong swimmer," I blurted out.

"You'll only be under for a second."

"I'm afraid I won't come back the same."

"The future is on hold until you do this."

I shut my eyes. I held my breath. I realized all paths led to the same place; the only difference between them was that some took longer than others and my best hope was moving as slowly as possible. The baptism wasn't for another week—I could live multiple lives before then. I told her I would be there, and she kissed me, and we kissed for a long time.

My parents didn't come to the baptism. They both worked on Sunday, and I'm glad they did. But Petey showed up. He bragged about how he had a fresh videotape just for this occasion. Gray clouds covered the sky like strips of gauze, holding back some terrible wound from the earth. People milled about on the rocky beach, filming with their phones, taking pictures, offering prayers. The pastor made the rounds, clapping people on the back and laughing, though I had no idea what there was to laugh about.

Petey elbowed my ribs. "Hey."

I turned to him.

"You should do something." He gestured at the river. "Do something for the camera while you're in there."

"What am I supposed to do?"

"I don't know. Something funny."

Before we could get into any specifics, Jess broke through the crowd and led me to the water's edge. Petey followed, red light of the camera blinking. We all gathered around the pastor.

The pastor wore dress pants and a white button-up shirt and a striped tie. He rolled up his pant legs, took off his shoes, then socks. He started talking, but I don't remember anything he said. I couldn't take my eyes off his feet. They were blindingly white, like slabs of bone. They seemed so slight and frail I thought they might snap under all his muscled weight. I was almost disappointed when they didn't.

And yet another thing I did not expect: The pastor waded into the river fully clothed. He sloshed forward until he was waist deep. I scanned the crowd for my fellow classmates. The woman was wearing jeans and a T-shirt, the old man khakis and a hoodie. Neither showed any signs of disrobing. I was suddenly painfully aware of my undersized bathing suit and my bare chest and how I alone had come prepared swim, they to die and be reborn. I hugged myself, mumbling something to Jess about being cold.

The woman was baptized first. Her jeans took on a darker shade as she glided into the water, and the bottom of her shirt billowed like a blooming flower. She didn't even shiver as she stood next to the rambling pastor. How was that even possible? It was as if she had been born from aquatic depths and was merely returning to her first home. I wanted to spit at her.

She crossed her arms. Closed her eyes. The pastor held her under for three seconds, each longer than the last. When she broke through the surface, bangs plastered against her forehead, she emerged radiant. The sky was still overcast, our surroundings more purgatorial waste than anything else, but her skin glowed as if backlit by some holy force. Everyone clapped as she made her way back to shore. Everyone except me, and probably Petey. She had come back different. She really had.

The pastor called my name. I glanced over my shoulder, at Petey, who only grinned and aimed the camera at me like a cannon. I took one lurching step toward the river and slipped on a loose rock; I would have fallen if Jess hadn't steadied me. With hunched shoulders, I shuffled toward the pastor. The river bottom was so slick I didn't even have to lift my feet off the ground.

Eventually, I made it. I turned around and stared at a crowd of mostly strangers who had come to watch me pretend to drown. I stood shivering and tried not to breathe in the briny stench flooding my nostrils. I tried to forget where I was and what this all meant.

The pastor said, "Are you committed?"

I nodded. That's all I could manage.

"Cross your arms."

I obeyed.

"Die to yourself," he said. "Be born anew."

"Wait," I whispered.

My guts slammed against my ribcage and I opened my mouth to scream, but it was too late. I was already buried.

How can I even begin to describe what happened in the murky dark? All the tightness eased out of my body. I tried to count the seconds, but soon realized that was pointless. I experienced time as the inanimate experience time; I could not detect its passing.

There was a resonant pounding, like a heartbeat, enveloping me in a cradle of sound. A strange thought rolled over me, maybe the only true thought I've ever had—here was the place I didn't even know I'd been looking for, the place where we choose whether or not to be born. The realization made me brave. I opened my eyes. Even though the water was muddy and the sky clouded, I swear I could see through it all, straight to the throne of heaven, where God sat watching on. But I couldn't see his face. Maybe he had no face. There were hands though, hands made up of infinite fingers, and on each of these was an expectation I could not meet.

I realized then how little love I had in my heart. I didn't want to be changed. I couldn't. I thrashed and struggled against the hands that held me. There was a sensation of rising, an oncoming grayness, and I was determined not to meet it. I kicked the pastor's spindly feet out from under him. I reached for his tie and pulled him under. We grappled amidst cold and pollution.

I struck out, again and again. Cartilage and bone crunched beneath my fists. Maroon tendrils of blood floated around us. Soon, my body grew heavy as I knew it would. I lashed out one last time and hit nothing but emptiness.

The pastor and I broke the surface at roughly the same time, both of us sputtering and coughing. His chest inflated and deflated like a great balloon. Two thin lines of watery blood dripped from his nostrils. His face had taken on an ugly shade of crimson.

He made a sudden move toward me, arms outstretched, mimicking the undead. Fingers flexing. Eyes on my neck. I believed, then, truly believed, he was going to strangle me.

Gasps and murmurs, a few shouts, floated to us from the beach. The pastor's bloodshot eyes widened, as if he remembered where he was and who he was. His rage passed from homicidal to a more acceptable kind—he slapped the water with his open palms and screamed at me. It was like he was trying to shout me out of existence. I almost asked him to yell louder.

I stumbled toward the shore, scrambled up the rocky beach on my hands and knees. No one in the crowd moved to help, probably because everything was happening so fast. Or maybe they had simply chosen to do what I would have done, which was nothing at all.

A presence loomed over me. My gaze flicked upward. Jess. Her lips were curled in embarrassment, maybe contempt, and her eyes were big and wet with tears, and even though she held out her hand, she seemed more like a wall than anything else, something designed to impede. How much shame was she willing to bear? The whole thing was incomprehensible. People talk about martyrs as if they're all dead, but here was a likeness which belonged in a gallery of miserable saints.

I said, "I can't."

"What?" Her voice quavered, but only slightly.

"I just can't."

I scrambled around her. I walked half-naked and shivering all the way to the street. Something soft hit me in the back. I turned around. There was a beach towel laying in a heap at my feet. There was Petey, shuffling in place.

"I'm out of film."

I wrapped myself in the towel. It smelled like sour smoke. I breathed deeply, let the scent fill my lungs.

"Did you at least get the whole thing?" I said.

"Yeah." Petey's dimples bulged as he grinned. "Let's watch the fucker."

Petey's basement was all shag carpet and plastic paneling designed to look like woodwork. We sat on beanbags amongst childhood relics—action figures and old board games, band posters wrinkled at the edges. We watched the video on the same VCR we used as kids.

I kept my phone close by. I stared at it as if it were a bomb.

"She won't call," Petey said. "Stop worrying and watch this shit."

"She might."

But I knew that was a lie.

So I turned my attention to the video. We watched the last few minutes over and over again. Petey slapped his knee and snickered at the end of each cycle.

"You sure as hell delivered," he said.

It was strange, seeing the pastor and me wrestle. We were little more than a tangle of limbs amidst disturbed water. There was a moment when we both went under, and all was quiet. Then we both burst forth, alive.

Petey had zoomed in on our expressions. He had captured the details, the essence of the sudden revival. Before he went under, the pastor had been poised, a man of goodwill and laughter. He emerged bedraggled, with bloodshot eyes and clenched fists, looking like some tormented demon, eager to inflict pain.

Me?

I came up pretty much the same.

Adam Scheffler

Hot Christ

The hokier the miracle the more
I believe in it, Jesus's face in a falafel,
the Virgin Mary in a vat
of mayonnaise.

True, we
work with what we've got:
statue, fake vomit,
YouTube video of beefy
Russian men slapping each other.

But we want to be dazzled
by the fine print
of instruction manuals.

We want to thrive in the 9-5 herd,
down-grimfaced falcons
of survival mode, while also
licking electric-frosted constellations
& spelling Christ's name with our tongues.

Aran Donovan

on the plane back to virginia

which is late, which is full, which is delayed again on the runway,
   waiting
for atc to finally verify the full weight of packed bags and people
pressed into thirty-two rows, i'm across the aisle from one of the flying
squirrels, the triple-a team out of Richmond, who has slung his leather
   mitt through
the straps of his carry-on to keep it close during the flight, and behind
an older couple, her thinning hair, his temple and glasses just
visible, the overhead light tracking a large-print thriller she tilts
   towards her
body. this is the only praying i do lately. i inventory us for mercy

Kathryn Bratt-Pfotenhauer

Darcy

I spend my Saturday night watching a man I liked
in middle school be bent over a table and spanked

with a riding crop in his father's play. He is an actor.
I am the audience. I have been given a ticket. I have

been assigned a seat. During the monologue
he looks at me with the intensity of recognition.

For a moment, I blush red as an ember, grateful
for the polypropylene mask. I have not had someone look at me

like that in a long time. I thought no one would look
at me like that again: straight to the meat of me, unsparing. I

had forgotten the lush hush of a black-
box theater, the cool anonymity under lights.

Being perceived unnerves me, but being ignored
is worse. Last Saturday, I saw the man

I thought I'd marry, and we passed by each other
and said nothing. He'd cut his hair. He did not look back.

It was clear he was not the man I had
loved. Desire made a door

of me. I stepped through the door. I packed my things
into a little brown suitcase and tried not to remember

we had talked about children at one point.
How we'd make such great parents.

A friend tells me that writing about the man is akin
to scraping ink from a burning house, and I'm inclined

to believe it. Not because he is beautiful to me anymore, but because
the metaphor is merely solid, and I've a penchant for taking what

was never mine to begin with. After all,
how many more original ways are there to say:

I loved you. You hurt me. And again.
You loved me. I hurt you. And again.

Mark Neely

Signal Crossing

To note the inevitable is a most steady terrible job
—Marianne Boruch

one best taken on by the poor
and bedraggled the bric-a-brac
hoarders closet historians living
in dead cars on the boulevard
bent on the why and the how
the internet says I have 13,667
days left to wiggle my toes they
shouldn't be too hard to frivol
away in the last few months I
took one million steps down
certain beige hallways I danced
through   drab   superstores
trailed my collie across the park
she's a high voltage wire her
tail sweeps the gutter her nose
splits the air into atoms I split
my time between hope and
regret once we drove sixteen
hours at night the ocean a
vast sigh in the darkness we
ate lobster for breakfast threw
ourselves from the rocks you
said only locals swim here we
screwed like bored royals two
lean immortals smoking in
bed no one could find us no

satellites arcing above my thoughts
ventured only two days in either
direction your blue Ford ticked
in the lot now they know my bad
habits my heart rate blood flow
they know we need t.p. broccoli
ketchup and rice they know we
have sex in the morning and for
how many minutes they track
stress levels tastes in pornography
my history of shame if I'm sick
or distracted they worry if I die it
costs them big money it all goes
in the tally they pay for this chair
where I study the planet's mood
swings or puzzle together shredded
love letters twisted root systems
old underground lines what I am
trying to say as we lurch through
this farcical century this morass
of amoral darkness this coral and
ivory fever I cut the red wire on my
dynamite vest tune into the lonely
the animal heaving inside me I
remember how letters took shape
on the board their fuzzy outlines
like the light around angels lank
aspens transliterating the wind
throw open a window flood this
dark wood with amber I am trying
to say we can change

Kathryn Kulpa

Where I'll Find You

Where do you want to live, I'd ask, and that would start the game. We had to play it every night, or we couldn't go to sleep. In our room with the dormer window and the pink-striped wallpaper and the twin beds with white ruffled canopies, until the allergy doctor said they attracted dust and our mother took them down. You had asthma.

I didn't have asthma. But we had to have everything alike, or it wouldn't be fair. Two beds exactly alike. But I'd still sneak into yours. We'd whisper, so we wouldn't get in trouble for talking after hours.

The game was better if we whispered.

I want to live in the meadow, you'd say. Like *The Runaway Bunny*. Maybe I'd be a bunny. In the morning I'd hop through golden-green baby grass, sweet and beaded with dew, and I'd nibble pink blossoms of clover. In the afternoon the grasses would sway in the wind, and bumblebees would buzz, low and lazy in the sun. I'd burrow a home for myself in the ground and line it with soft grass, with yellow daisies and pink coneflowers, and nap away the hot day. At night I'd dance a rabbit dance under the stars. I'd send kisses to the rabbit in the moon, and he would send them back to me.

And where do you *not* want to live, you'd ask me.

I don't want to live at the beach, I'd say. I don't want to spend all day making a perfect sand castle and have some mean boy knock it over. I don't want to have a seagull steal my lunch. I don't want to jump into the waves and get water up my nose and then get stung by a jellyfish and have my mom get vinegar from the snack bar and pour it over the sting and have to stay out of the water for the rest of the day, lying on a gritty towel reading a waterlogged book and getting a sunburn so bad I can't bend my legs and have to stick my face in the freezer.

☾

It was the best game, a game only you and I knew. We could stop the game at any time and go back to it the next night. We still can.

Where do you want to visit just for one day, I ask.

I want to visit the city, you say. As a tourist, a dumb tourist who stares up at skyscrapers and says *Wow, look at those buildings!* I want to yell *Taxi!* to flag down a taxi and then sit in the front seat because I'm a tourist. *Take me to the Statue of Liberty*, I'll say. *Take me to the Empire State.* I want to visit Times Square, like *The Cricket in Times Square.* It's my Big Apple, and I want to chew it up and spit it out on the dirty sidewalk and not care who has to clean it up or if anybody does, because I'll be gone. Because I'm a tourist and I'm only there for one day and what do I care how I leave things for everybody else?

You're breathing too fast. Some machine on the side of the bed beeps, and I'm afraid a nurse will come and tell me to leave, but no one does. The news is full of shortages. Walkouts. Ambulances turned away at the doors. Slow down, I tell you. I give you a tiny cube from a melting cup of ice.

You ask me: Where do you want to go and stay forever and ever?

And I say: I want to go to the forest and stay there forever and ever. I want to live in the oldest forest with the oldest old-growth trees, trees so tall they tickle the clouds. The forest floor is dense with pine needles, and when you walk on them it's like walking on deep pile carpet. I want to gather mayapples in the spring and pine cones in the fall. I want to brew tea from dandelion leaves and make myself a bed of the softest moss, moss so deep and green it could only grow in a forest this old, this untouched, and you'll be there, too. We'll lie in our beds of moss, under a canopy of stars, and all the cats we've loved and all the dogs we've loved will curl up there beside us, and all we'll hear is the wind sighing through the pine branches, whispering us to sleep, and the wind says *shhhh*, and the wind says *shhhh*.

And you're asleep. Your thin hand, purple with IV bruises, rises and falls on your chest. I walk away, silent as the softest moss, my feet sinking into deep pine needles on the bleached tile floor.

Sharmin Rahman

Pumpkin Pie

It's September and I'm heading to a tiki bar in the Upper West Side to meet Blondie and her friends. I stop at Duane Reade beforehand to get a bottled iced tea. I guzzle it down with an Adderall and Xanax, a self-made cocktail I store in Ziploc bags that keep me going every day. I haven't been sleeping much lately.

I can't figure out how Blondie's friends feel at any given moment because of all the Botox gashed into their faces. They've perfected their mannerisms around each other as though they're acting in a play. One girl has a British accent, which seems to impress everyone, so I start speaking in one, too, but the Brit gets offended. They bore me, so I walk up to a guy and I try to get him to buy me a drink.

"Well, don't you smell sexy," I say to him. "Like fresh-baked pumpkin pie."

It's true; the whole bar smells of it. I don't get my drink. Instead he walks away from me. I can't blame him—I look atrocious. I don't have enough money to split the bill, so I leave the bar.

The pills must've done a number on me because the smell of pumpkin pie follows me as I head east to Central Park. The smell reminds me of the coming fall.

In the fall, since childhood, my older sister and I religiously baked pumpkin pie together. We'd turn over every couch cushion looking for coins, go to the market to buy canned pumpkins, and take the spices from my mother's cabinet. She'd fume at us, but she'd always been a bitter woman, usually about her regrettable shopping habits, which led to debt collectors calling her at work.

When we didn't want to be home, we played handball in our schoolyard. I didn't fit in at school. It was hard for me to make friends.

One day, one of the older boys approached me. I was seven at the time, holding the cans we just bought.

"Troll," he sneered as he knocked the cans out of my hands.

"He's the real troll, sister," my sister reassured me later.

She was one of the few who made it to college. After that, she got a fancy investment job. She worked through the night and I saw her less. She bought her own apartment, and the debt collectors stopped calling my mother.

In Central Park, I start to doze off on a bench when I notice a man's ghostly figure illuminating in front of me. His skin, the color of baked walnuts, creases all sorts of ways when he takes a deep breath. His eyelashes flutter before he opens his eyes, revealing a mesmerizing honey color. Then he gets up and walks in a quick pace, which energizes me. I follow him.

Outside the park, a man and woman join him. He kisses the man and introduces himself to the woman as Max.

Max then notices me and smiles as though he recognizes a familiar face.

"Why don't you come with us?" he insists.

Everyone nods in unison. I don't decline.

We hop into the 6 train heading to the East Village. On the crowded platform, an old man I'd seen around plays "Yellow Submarine" on his violin. We listen and Max holds my hand, guiding me through a waltz. Everyone quietly dances next to us, like characters in a mise-en-scène.

At a dilapidated punk bar, Max buys us cheap beer and peels band stickers off the table. He sticks them on his nails and dances around while we cheer him on. None of us go to the bathroom the whole time in fear we'll miss out on a laugh.

At last call, the smell of pumpkin pie reincarnates again. Why couldn't I bring myself to ask Max? What was I afraid of, anyway? To act on impulse again?

"I keep smelling pumpkin pie, and it's not even fall yet," I tell Max, perplexed.

His eyes light up and he tells me, "I'm a pastry chef at Magnolia Bakery. I've been perfecting a new pumpkin pie recipe for this fall."

I tell Max that with my sister, I'd whisk the puree in a bowl held against my arms, pretending I was a chef, too. I always messed up the crust, so I let her take that responsibility.

Max picks up my hand and directs my fingers.

There was always a hollowness in the way my sister moved as she'd wallow her fingers into the crust, shaping it like clay. When I'd inquire, she'd say "There are important things in the world to worry about." And while we waited for the pie to bake, we danced like maniacs to the Beatles until we capsized on the couch and no worries existed.

That was all before that fall morning, almost a year ago, when I got the news that my sister had drowned herself and my world upended. "They'll cremate her," my mother told me over the white cloth by the East River. "You can keep the ashes," she said as a gesture, but I didn't need any more proof my sister was gone.

There are some things I don't allow myself to think of. How long my sister gasped for air in the briny water. Her glossy hair and how she tore up bread up for the sidewalk pigeons, now all of her washed away by the water and burned to ashes.

I call Max a beautiful saint and I thank him for the evening.

"We'll see each other again," he says. "There's a cosmic understanding between us."

Outside, the gold streetlights twinkle in the night sky. I take the subway home and go to bed. In the morning, I wake up from a dreamless sleep and take the Ziploc bags out of my nightstand and dump the contents into the trash.

I walk to Magnolia to see Max again. I wait outside for the shop to open. Finally, an old man with hairy hands comes and rattles the grates of the bakery open. I ask him about Max.

He tells me that there is no one named Max at the bakery.

What about the pumpkin pie?

"Pumpkin pie?" he says. "It's August." His wide laugh reveals his upper gum tissue.

I stand silent.

"What are you really looking for?" he asks me in a peculiar way.

"Nothing," I say. And when I say that out loud, I am confronted with the fact that I am lying.

My eyes fill with clouds of water, burning. The violet sky recedes behind the sun born over the smokey city. There is no aroma of pumpkin pie anymore, just the sweltering odor of the rotting garbage from summers' end.

Susanna Goldfinger

Cool Girls Don't Tell

SUSANNA GOLDFINGER

ONCE UPON A TIME I WAS A SMALL MOUSE. WELL—
I WAS A COLLEGE STUDENT IN PHILADELPHIA BUT I
FELT LIKE A MOUSE.

EVERY MORNING I WOKE
UP AND EVERY NIGHT I
WENT TO BED, TERRIFIED.

THE BOOKS I WAS
READING DIDN'T HELP.

I BECAME FRIENDS WITH A GIRL IN MY LITERARY THEORY CLASS WHO WASN'T TERRIFIED. SHE WAS COOL. SHE HAD A TATTOO OF A SNAKE EATING ITS TAIL

ON HER SHOULDER. SHE SAID IT WAS A REFERENCE TO NIETZSCHE'S IDEA OF ETERNAL RETURN.

SHE TOOK ME TO A DARK BAR IN CENTER CITY WHERE THEY DIDN'T CHECK ID. WE DRANK GIN AND TONICS AND TALKED ABOUT LITERATURE AND SEX.

SHE TOLD ME SHE WAS SLEEPING WITH A FEW
DIFFERENT OLDER MEN — NOT-STUDENTS. I COULD
ONLY IMAGINE SUCH THINGS. MY MOUSEY BODY WAS
AT THAT TIME UNTOUCHED.

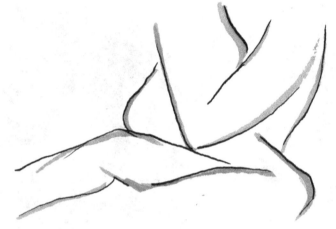

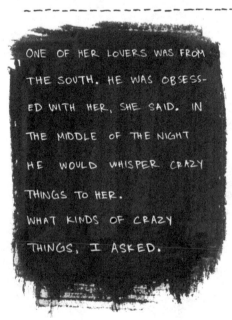

ONE OF HER LOVERS WAS FROM
THE SOUTH. HE WAS OBSESS-
ED WITH HER, SHE SAID. IN
THE MIDDLE OF THE NIGHT
HE WOULD WHISPER CRAZY
THINGS TO HER.
WHAT KINDS OF CRAZY
THINGS, I ASKED.

HE WANTED TO LIVE WITH
HER IN A HOUSE ON A
LAKE.

A DOOR TO A NEW WORLD WAS OPENING.

I KNEW I DIDN'T BELONG BUT MAYBE I COULD SLIP BY UNNOTICED. I WAS JUST A LITTLE MOUSE.

THAT NIGHT I WENT TO BED WITH A HEAD FULL OF WORDS AND PICTURES.

A FEW DAYS LATER MY
FRIEND GOT A CALL FROM
HER SOUTHERN LOVER.

HE SAID

THE HOUSE

ON

THE LAKE

WAS READY

FOR THEM.

IT WAS HIS PARENTS' HOUSE AND IT WAS
AVAILABLE BECAUSE HE HAD MURDERED THEM.

ARE YOU GOING TO CALL
THE POLICE? I ASKED.

SHE SHOOK HER HEAD.
SHE DIDN'T SAY WHY BUT
I KNEW:

COOL
GIRLS
DON'T
TELL

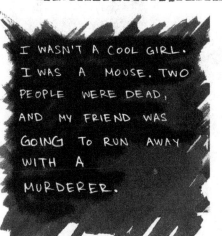

I WASN'T A COOL GIRL.
I WAS A MOUSE. TWO
PEOPLE WERE DEAD,
AND MY FRIEND WAS
GOING TO RUN AWAY
WITH A
MURDERER.

TLDR:
IT DIDN'T MATTER.
HE WAS QUICKLY CAUGHT
AND CONVICTED. THEY
NEVER MADE IT TO
THE HOUSE ON THE LAKE.

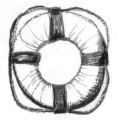

I'VE BEEN TRYING TO WRITE THIS STORY FOR TWENTY YEARS. I'M NOT A COOL GIRL BUT STILL IT'S BEEN HARD TO TELL. I DON'T TRUST MY OWN MEMORY.

I WONDER IF MAYBE IT WASN'T COOL GIRL CODE THAT KEPT MY FRIEND QUIET. MAYBE IT WAS FEAR.

FUNNY HOW I NEVER ASSIGN FEAR TO ANYONE ELSE.

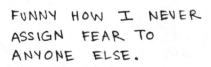

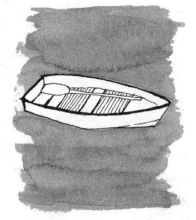

I LEFT PHILADELPHIA YEARS AGO BUT THE OTHER NIGHT I DREAMT I WAS WALKING THERE ON A RAINY NIGHT.

THERE WAS A SHADOW IN A DOORWAY. SOMEHOW I KNEW IT WAS HIM. DO YOU KNOW WHO I AM? HE CALLED OUT. I NODDED BUT DIDN'T BREAK MY STRIDE.

IN MY DREAM I THOUGHT, HE'S GOT THE WRONG GIRL. HE THINKS I'M MY FRIEND. SHE'S THE ONE HE WANTS. IN DREAMS AND STORIES THEY LIVE FOREVER IN THE HOUSE ON THE LAKE.

/end

Alyx Chandler

First Kiss

Just a popcorn machine and metal cash kit.
Every Saturday, that's how we had to do it—

crank our cuteness hell-bent into cash
at the Limestone County Flea Market.

Butter people up in bidding wars, burst
their wallets open. If something wasn't

at the flea market, it wasn't anywhere.
Kids, don't let anyone touch you! Or

the money! Then our moms would disappear
into the swarm of shoppers, dart straight

to the garment racks, our school clothes
hidden in mannequin land. We ate ourselves

sick, quick pleasantries in checkered bags,
quarters pocketed as popcorn hit glass hard.

We stole dollars from purses, salt from
each other's mouths—tonguing capitalism

in a tiny, greasy booth, tasting it in everything.
What we craved: to be free between stalls,

raid plastic tubs, haggle for doll heads and
broken unicycles, to dip our claws into

bulk-sized buckets, marble eyeballs. Hot kernels
turning cold, rolling around our mouths

like a reminder. Old maids, they're called:
the dangerous ones that slip past lips and

crack teeth. The ones that won't ever pop,
no matter how high we turn up the heat.

Martha E. Snell

Reminds Me of Love

Ripe purple plum,
I hold your round body.

You are smooth in my palm,
smooth in my mouth.

I bite through your black
silk gown, and juice

bolts my tongue. Sweetness—
my lips, my chin, my fingers—

you cling to my skin. Pulp
the color of sunsets almost

done, almost like love, dark
maroon of placentas.

Sandra Fees

Self-Portrait as Bioluminescence

If I could empathy with color,
    I would kindle blue-green, green-

blue like a clusterwink snail that
        emits a warning, a lusting. There,
    in a depth of ocean, the floor

would plummet beneath human
reach. I would flash red-eyed

like the dragonfish, offering
    a rebuke to the trawler's net
        and miner's drill. Bellied with light,

like the sun or some tiny god,
        lush and luminous, I would know how
    to survive this darkness, how to let
there be light. I would be

some creature I've never been.

Nancy Carol Moody

Ruby

It's true I fell in love
at the raptor center.

Feathers slinking dark,
exhaling the skank
of long-dead meat.
Quasimodo hunker.
The brutal convolutions
of her face, red
as a hibiscus on fire.

Do you know
a vulture's stomach
is a pouch of pure acid?
That she defecates
on herself to kill the bacteria
clinging to her legs?
That her baldness keeps
dead flesh from sticking
when she withdraws her head
from the rectum of a carcass?

But it's merely academic lust,
this laying-out of facts—
it was her eye that made me
fall so hard.

Ruby

Eye of cappuccino.
Eye made from chocolate melt.
Eye so soft
and tender with her gaze
it didn't reflect
my own astringency back.

Shane Kowalski

Comfort

Your boss asks you to help him with his marriage. So, you sleep with his wife. Her name is Lucinda. She tells you your boss is a shell of a man, is rotten, won't let her buy a tortoise, sleeps with a hundred-dollar bill taped to the back of his head. You know. But you don't say you know. This is an intimacy. Lucinda pulls you in and kisses the back of your head. As you hold each other in the night, in your boss's bed, you think you can hear all the life in the deep of the sea sing a song that won't make sense until someone else's lifetime.

Zoa Coudret

A little martyrdom

There is a breathlong moment before the needle jabs when you think, *Maybe the piercer will nick a vital artery, maybe this will send me to hell* & you wonder if you are only doing this because your partner has broken up with you & you want to choose the way you hurt, which it really does as metal slides through skin, pain stuns nostril to brain & you suffer, Christlike, for a few seconds—long enough to wonder *Would Jesus have gotten a nose ring if there'd been a piercing shop in Nazareth? Definitely a tattoo, perhaps a "MOM" heart or a realistic portrait of his father, burning bush, all black & gray, flames rising from biceps to shoulder*—before your eyes clench & tears flow like holy water on a baby's bald head, the little blood you lost will replenish, unlike your self-esteem when a pale selfie reveals the niobium bar stuck through the bridge of your nose, misplaced stigmata, you wish someone were here to pose with you to make your ex jealous, make them think you're thriving, because you crave their regret, want them to see you strong and unbothered, desire so much more than what a little piece of metal can give.

Laura Leigh Morris

The Pantry Store

The phone rang at eleven, too late for anything good. Miller sat on the couch, beer in hand, a few dead soldiers on the end table, eyes closed. Benji was in his bed, the only one in the house. She'd fallen asleep watching a movie, something she said was too little for an almost-twelve-year-old but then couldn't turn away from, refusing to go to bed even when she nodded off before the end. He'd carried her there when the credits rolled, arms and legs spilling over his grip, almost too big to carry. Miller hit talk before the ring could wake her.

"I need you to come in," Stella said. She sounded exhausted. Loud voices in the background, the ding of the Pantry Store's register. "I'm falling asleep standing up, and there's no one to work tonight."

Miller looked toward the bedroom door, Benji's snores trailing through the house. He was always shocked a little girl could make such an awful noise. She'd been like that even as a toddler, making noises louder than most grown men. "I've got Benji."

"Take her to her mom's. I need you."

Stella had been relying on him more recently, letting him make the dairy order each week, teaching him how to make cigarette and beer orders based on the shifts at the mines and drill sites. He'd already taken over the grocery aisle, rearranging so the potted meat and Spam were the first things you saw, right beside loaves of white bread, edging them both closer to the pork rinds—a full meal at the end of a long shift at the mines or bar. Stella said they were flying off the shelves and gave him permission to make whatever other changes he wanted. Last week, she said if he kept up the good work he might see a promotion to assistant manager in his future. And Miller needed the money. He'd hadn't kept up with child support payments the past few months, sending April less than half of what he owed. And he'd only been able to give her that much because he hadn't paid his other bills. He'd received a third notice on the water bill recently and had sent them a check for twenty dollars, nowhere near what he owed. He expected a second notice on the gas bill any day now.

The promotion would let him get Benji on a regular schedule again, too. For the past six months, he'd been working nights and had only seen Benji when he got out of the Pantry Store early enough to rush to Brickton Elementary and talk to her through the chain -link fence before the morning bell. There, she always asked when she could spend the night again, and he always replied, "Soon," though soon never got any closer. It was dumb luck that Stella had wanted to train the new guy on nights this weekend and April had agreed to let Benji stay, though only after Miller had promised to catch up on child support with his next paycheck. Not that he would, but he figured spending time with Benji was more important than telling the truth.

"Miller," Stella said. "I hate to say it, but this is the sort of thing I'd expect of an assistant manager."

"I can be there in twenty."

"Great." There was relief in her voice. When he got the promotion, Miller would do something for Stella. She was good people.

He shook Benji's shoulder, but she didn't move. "We have to go," he said. She mumbled something but didn't wake. He shook her again, and she rolled away, whining. Miller grabbed her, pillow and blanket and all, and bundled her into the truck. She curled up in the corner, her thumb snaking into her mouth, a habit he and April had tried to stop years ago, but tonight he was glad to see a little bit of childhood sneaking out. From this evening's constant eye rolls and the way she jumped whenever her phone dinged, it was clear she now lived in some pre-teen land where hugs from Dad and a promise of candy after dinner meant nothing against the promise of texting with friends all evening. She even tried to get him to override some of April's rules, especially the one about no makeup before thirteen. But he'd said no, not so much out of loyalty to his ex-wife, but more because he couldn't imagine his little girl looking as grown as she was trying to act.

Outside the Pantry Store, he stopped long enough to make a little bed for her on the truck's bench seat—setting her pillow against the door, tucking the comforter around her whole body. She woke, squinted up at him, and mumbled, "Lemme sleep."

"It's OK, Bug." He smoothed her hair from her face. "You sleep. I'll be watching you." He was parked directly in front of the store's glass doors, where he could keep an eye on the truck from behind the register. He'd rather have her inside but figured it would be more comfortable out here. Besides, the store would be pretty much empty until four-thirty a.m., when the old timers began to arrive in search of coffee and other old men who couldn't sleep and wanted to hash out the same arguments day after day.

Inside, Stella already had her coat on, a bag slung over her shoulder. Her hair was unwashed and stringy, gunmetal gray roots showing through the dye job. If possible, she looked even thinner than usual.

"You OK?" Miller asked.

"Hi to you, too." She yawned. "Anderson quit. Called up and said he wasn't coming in anymore. I worked a triple, took a nap in the store room earlier."

"Shit. You should have called."

"I did." She was heading out from around the counter, pulling car keys from her pocket.

"Sleep as long as you need. I can hold down the fort."

The night shift was boring at the best of times. On weekends, a few drunks would stop by when the bars closed at two, begging for more beer, though he couldn't sell it. Not at that hour. They always tried to cajole him, and he always shook his head, sending them away with a smile. Other than that, Miller spent most nights restocking and rearranging. Tonight, he ignored the half-empty shelves and kept his eye on the truck. A little after one, Benji sat up, looked around, and disappeared below the line of the dashboard again. He hadn't seen her since.

Miller wondered if he could convince her not to tell April about sleeping here. Even if she agreed, she'd slip at some point and April would be mad as hell. Still, if she kept quiet through tomorrow's call with her mom, he'd have her the whole weekend. Stella would expect him to work tomorrow night, too, especially if he wanted that promotion. Maybe he could talk her into working part of the shift. Then, he could put Benji in the truck again when she was already asleep. Maybe even get Stella to come in at four-thirty or five, early enough that Benji wouldn't know she'd been anywhere but bed.

It was after three when he noticed the commotion, a pair of drunk teens weaving across the lot, arms around one another's shoulders, singing at the tops of their lungs. One of their faces was covered in a thick layer of peach fuzz, the other with a full beard on a baby face. They walked past the truck without looking inside, and Miller prayed Benji would remain asleep. In the store, they ignored Miller and went directly to the beer cooler, pulling out a case of Natural Light. Their energy was off. They were strangely quiet, their eyes sliding from side to side.

"Sorry," Miller said when they shoved the beer across the counter. "No can do."

The hairy one slid an ID toward him, probably fake.

"Doesn't matter," he said. "I can't sell after midnight."

The other hacked up a loogie and spat on the floor. He looked Miller in the eye, a challenge, and said, "Fucking backward redneck store," in a thick, local drawl. Miller couldn't place his face, wondered if he knew his dad. He'd probably sold him gas and a pack of smokes. He held the boy's gaze, waited. They stood their ground for another second, then turned and walked out the store.

Miller froze as they approached the truck. The boys stopped and peered in the window. Miller's heart pounded, his hands shook. The bearded one beat his fist against the passenger side window. Benji sat up and looked around wildly. Miller vaulted the counter. "Hey," he yelled, pushing through the doors. "You boys need to get on your way."

Benji called out to him. Miller didn't turn to her, was busy staring at the two drunks who were sizing him up. He was taller and broader than them, but they had youth and liquid courage on their side. He held his palm toward Benji, hoped she understood he was saying stop, stay, do not unlock the door. Peach fuzz walked to the front of the truck, pantomimed humping the bumper, laughed and stared at Benji. Miller grabbed his shoulder, turned him around, and jabbed him once in the nose, hard enough to make his eyes water and his nostrils pour blood. He could have stopped there. He'd made his point. Instead, Miller popped him in the nose again and pushed him. The kid tripped over the parking bumper, fell backward, and his head bounced off the asphalt. Miller pulled his leg back to kick the kid, when the other boy yelled out, and Miller stopped, heard Benji calling for him.

The bearded boy walked toward him slowly, warily.

"You want some?" Miller held his arms wide, beckoned with his fingers. "I'll fuck you up, boy."

Benji was screaming inside the truck, rattling the handle.

"Don't you move, Bug," he called. He didn't look away from the boy in front of him, and kept an eye on the one on the ground. "Stay right there, baby."

"Fuck," the kid on the ground said, holding his nose, the word muffled by blood. "Asshole's crazy."

The bearded kid kept his eyes on Miller but squatted, pulled his friend up by the arm. "My dad'll have something to say about this."

Miller squinted, tried to place him. Couldn't. Didn't matter. "And your dad'll get an earful about how his drunk son likes scaring little girls in the middle of the night."

"We was just playing." He pointed at his friend, who was still trying to stifle the flow from his nose. "That wasn't playing."

"Try it again and you'll see how much I play." Though the fight had gone out of him. He wished they'd go away and take the nagging feeling he'd completely fucked up with them.

They took a step backward.

Red and blue lights flashed from the parking lot of the funeral home across the street, and the siren rang out, one sharp whoop. Miller prayed for one of the cops he knew. These boys couldn't be more than sixteen or seventeen. Not legal in any sense. The bearded one started yelling as soon as Andrew Kent stepped out of the car. He had a bad mustache, thinning hair, a potbelly. He and Miller had gone to high school together.

"Everything OK here?" he asked, his palm out to the kid yelling at him, other hand on the butt of his gun.

"We weren't doing nothing, and that asshole hit Ernie," the boy yelled. Ernie stood up straight, blood now drying on his chin, his nose already discolored and swelling. He reached up, touched the back of his head. His fingers came away bloody.

Benji began to scream again, and Miller hurried to open the truck door. She launched herself into his arms, crying more than any of this warranted, though Miller had to admit it must be scary waking up in the middle of the night in a parking lot and seeing your dad beating up on people. "It's OK, baby," Miller said into Benji's ear, her legs wrapped around his waist as though she were six instead of eleven, her arms locked around his neck. "Everything's fine."

"You see what he did?" the hairy one screamed at Andrew, gesturing toward Ernie. "He's nuts."

Andrew glanced at Miller, then leaned toward the two boys, sniffing loudly. "You two been drinking? You got any ID?"

Hairy backed up, closing his mouth. "Seriously?"

"Seriously," Andrew said.

Miller turned away from the scene, shushing his daughter, bouncing her like a baby. She wiped her face against the shoulder of his T-shirt, and he breathed in her anxious sweat, the sour oniony smell that comes with puberty. Slowly, her sobs subsided. When he turned back to Andrew, the two boys were walking across the lot, throwing dirty looks toward Miller.

"Why don't you get yourself a pop?" Miller said to Benji. She looked up at him, the tears still there, a bit of wariness in her gaze. "It's OK," he said and nodded. "They won't be back." She jumped down, ran into the store.

"What the hell?" Andrew asked.

"I know." Miller shook his head. "It was stupid."

"You're lucky," Andrew said. "Damned lucky those boys were drinking. If not, this could've turned into a shit show."

"The hairy one said he's gonna tell his dad," Miller said. "You know him?"

Andrew stared at the boys' backs, one hand scratching at his caterpillar mustache. "Shit."

"What?"

"Those are Donnie Weaver's boys."

Donnie was the guy who threatened the ref at middle school basketball games, who'd argue with you until you admitted you were wrong just so he'd shut the hell up. Miller never had liked him much. His only hope was the boys were more worried about being drunk than the harm he'd done. Shit. Shit. Shit.

"Tell me what happened," Andrew said. "Let's see if we can get ahead of this."

Miller rubbed his face and shook his head, didn't have it in him at the moment. Benji stood just inside the glass doors, her nose pressed against the glass.

Andrew waited, but Miller stayed silent. If he talked now, some mangled version of the story would make its way through Brickton by morning and get back to April by early afternoon. Then, he wouldn't get a second night with Benji.

"You need to watch your ass," Andrew said when the silence had drawn out between them. "And I'm not gonna say a thing about what the hell your girl's doing out here in the middle of the night. Or the fact that she was obviously sleeping in your truck. Not a word." He went back to his car, turned the lights off, and pulled out of the lot.

Miller took a deep breath and let a sob escape before turning to Benji, who stared at him through the glass. She looked like his little girl again, not the tween he'd tried to entertain all evening.

Miller walked to the store. She backed away from the door, all the way to the counter. He went to the cooler and pulled out a can of Pepsi. From the candy aisle he grabbed a Snickers bar. He handed them both to Benji and guided her to the chair behind the counter. He crouched in front of her. "You OK, Bug?" She stared at the floor. "Don't worry. Those boys are gone. I promise they won't hurt you." She still didn't look at him. She was exhausted, confused, probably still shaken. These sorts of things were scary to kids. "You're safe in here. I'll get your pillow and blanket, and you can sleep right here, OK?"

"I want to go home," she whispered, chin on her chest.

"I have to work, but we'll go home first thing in the morning."

"Call Mom," she said, louder, and looked at him. "She'll come get me."

"I'm not calling your mom." Too loud. Benji cringed, her chin quivered. Shit. "I promise you're safe," he said more softly and smoothed her hair away from her face. She jumped under his touch, but he left his hand there an extra second. "I'm gonna make you a bed right here, and when you wake up, it'll be time to go. I won't let anything happen to you."

He waited for her to say something or nod, but she didn't move. Miller sighed and stood. He grabbed her bedding from the truck and made a nest for her on the floor behind the counter, which he should have done to begin with. She sat, hugged the pillow to her chest. She still hadn't opened her pop and candy bar.

Miller squatted in front of her, said, "I know that was scary. It was for me, too." She wouldn't look at him. He took a deep breath. "I know when bad things happen you want to tell your Mom, but I'm gonna ask you not to tell her this time." She didn't respond, but at least she looked at him. He took that as a good sign. "We'll keep it between us, OK? Our little secret." She blinked. "What do you say?" Eyes wide, Benji stared but didn't say a word.

Miller walked back to the candy section. He grabbed a pack of gum, a Hershey bar, and some Starburst. He laid them before her, an offering. She stared at them. He lifted her chin. She jumped. Damn those boys. Scaring his little girl. Young lady, he corrected himself. She was growing up, and there was no better time to acknowledge it than the present.

"Benji," he said, making his voice a little deeper, shifting his tone so she'd hear how important his words were. "I've been amazed at how much you've grown up since you last spent the night. I was thinking of you as a little girl, but tonight I've realized you're a young woman. And I want to treat you that way. I'm asking this only because I know you're grown up enough to do it: can we make what happened tonight our secret?" He paused, but she said nothing. "Of course," he added, "growing up comes with other advantages: makeup, painting your nails." He could see the cogs turning in her head. "Only if you want to, of course."

She touched the candy with her fingers, looked up, and nodded. Her eyes were focused somewhere behind him, but he saw a glimmer in them.

Miller let go of her chin and stood. "Good." She stared at the floor again, still didn't open the candy or pop. Those boys really had scared her. Little assholes. Like their father. They'd deserved what Miller had done, but he didn't guess that was a good excuse. He shook his head. Nothing he could do about it now. He rubbed his hands together, looked out over the rows of goods in the store, bet if he put the Slim Jims and bags of peanuts closer to the beer cooler they'd jump off the shelf. Miller could feel it in his bones: He'd be assistant manager soon. Then he'd make things right.

Ian C. Williams

Not Even Robert Stack Could Figure Out Why I'm Here, So You Can Quit Asking

Even now, if you check the Google Maps Street View,
you can see where the tires scrawled my signature

in the gravel and dirt on the corner of Vinegar Hill Road,
when, at seventeen, I panicked and plowed across

a lane of late-afternoon traffic and into the sudden quiet
that suffocates after car horn and the grit of my own teeth.

Before my father hushes me into the passenger seat.
    Before we drove home in silence.

As the earth has scratched its long, pink scars in my shins
with its thistles and bark, I have etched lines

among these hills. My name is engraved in its soil.
When I dug up my ankles and ripped my limbs from this place,

I left something behind. And too often
that something echoes after me. It tells me to come home.

Ian C. Williams

I've Always Been a Sucker for a Good Pick Slide

This was when we spent summer camps at a distance,
distracted by girls as the green wing of June
filtered through the sugar maples above us,
when you had your friends and I had my loneliness
and I confessed to you my addiction, hoping to borrow
some of the confidence carried in your grin—
when you forgot about me.

Years later, when you called me over to your car—
its leather mixing with your frosted breath,
the growl of guitars crawling from underneath
the hairline crack in your self-assurance—
and you unexpectedly expressed your regret after a breakup—
as if asking for forgiveness—as if you knew,
in two years, this woman would marry me—
I think we were almost friends.

It's not every day that I think about you,
but it's often enough. Often enough to notice your absence
from my life. Often enough to see that break
in the forest canopy where we could have been brothers—
that break that shares your outline.

Clayton Adam Clark

Triangulate

The tornado siren
megaphone I've yet
to spot in all my walking
but (can hear clear and north
enough to) believe it somewhere
between home and the train
yard, woodpeckers drumming
trees with spongy skulls
this spring, some hailing mates
about a nesting site
and sometimes after timber
pests (and I am never
knowing which is which),
the nest balancing on
a power line's attachment
to my home with nothing
inside it and a squirrel
pup I found on the driveway,
hairless and dead beneath
an elm branch, plus how I
don't know who sounds that siren,
(not really) but I expect
to hear about a threat
when I need to (even
if I don't always retreat
to the basement when warned),
which means I make disaster
have to do with me

before I give it mind
and/or body, and maybe
also those bagpipes Friday
afternoons I hear
at work in the yard, a neighbor
playing songs I know
(from funerals) and feeling
urged to thank them for all
these dead dredged up (and somehow
also returned to me
(both tonic and refrain))
from someplace (I hadn't
known I am) but can't
home in on which house
the dirges issue from.

Clayton Adam Clark

Lesser Midwest Earthquakes

1.
In my sleep, I feel the trains connect, the violence
of their coupling at the intermodal transit center
and its downhill emanation through my neighborhood,
                    home, these bedposts.

2.
It was the picture frame in contact
with hardwood floor, its breaking

glass received by my temporal lobe,
that woke me in a minor earthquake.

The felt area is far-reaching on account
of rigid bedrock beneath the soil,

so I was prepared for this, annually
crouched beneath a school desk,

the New Madrid Seismic Zone
asleep but threatening.

3.
I caught myself rising with a craving for news reports of upturned
        asphalt and the chimneys toppled, not a man with stitches
        across his brow and the glass angel that descended from a shelf
        to disfigure him.

4.
Limestone bluffs crumbled
          into the Mississippi River
                    two hundred years ago
when the New Madrid moved most,
          the forests wasted and soil liquefactive.
                    Boat captains reported the shockwaves
shoved the Mississippi backwards
          several minutes; scientists today
                    offer diverging hypotheses.

5.
It's all in your head, the phantom quake,
though it's under your feet you feel it.

6.
When I first moved here, I was
          always hearing the engines chunk
across the River Des Peres, the whistles

          of metal abrading metal, and don't now.
My amygdala still activates sometimes
          when the train yard *booms* and shakes me

more than usual but with fewer
          threats erupting in my frontal lobe:
a bombing or another accident

          at the chemical plant nestled upstream?

7.
Bourne above the aulacogen,   the earth is weaker here,
mechanically speaking. We could   expect a fantastic loss
of life and shelter if   the 1811-12 New Madrid earthquakes
hit today because we are   so many more, so densely living.

8.
Like any faults, ours here are deep-seated
and old. Inside me I have both the place

where I want to see the rivers backward
and the earth gaping at my feet, destruction
returning people to earth, and the other
that issues discomfort to my intestines
when I imagine who and how we'd hurt.
They may not be so far apart, these places.

9.
Or I am, always at least a little, fearful and dying to see something I
    can't believe.

10.
The news has had me
waiting for skyfall,
and then there's how
I learn to sort out
what is and isn't.
It's all in the basement,
the water and canned food,
first aid supplies, which
means I sometimes feel
equipped for intraplate
activity but not its after.

11.
Carrying broken glass out to the garbage
the next morning, I found the trash can

overturned and credited the earthquake
more magnitude until I saw the strewn

food containers and claw marks in
a plastic bag torn open by raccoons.

Sherrie Flick

Like Rain

Mark held his hand out flat like a stop sign. "Wait," he said, and like magic, she did.

Julie was waiting. Mark knew this meant she thought he had something to say, that he had a chance.

"What?" she said, like a pistol shot, tapping her foot once, which made the bookshelf in their entryway wobble. Julie's face was blank, faceless, completely paper plate.

"I just wanted to say I don't want you to leave like this. I don't want it to be so ... trite?" Mark said. He lifted his arms into a shrug, tried to look eager and charming. He was hemming and hawing or hedging his bets. He could never get cliches right. Mark wasn't good at improv, unlike Julie, who could grab the spatula someone handed her on stage and break into a meaningful song about it that included dance steps. "I mean you're storming out of the house," he continued. "*Storming.* Not very mature. Did you think of the cat, the plants, me?" He did think better of putting himself at the center. "Did you think of the cat, Julie?" Mark picked up their big fat tabby, Jimbo, who didn't look in Julie's direction but just stared at the jade plant in the opposite corner.

One day Julie fried falafel in their cast-iron skillet, oily steam rising around her face. The next day Mark told her about Dorothy. The next day was now.

"I've thought about the cat, Mark. Fuck the cat. I'm out of here," Julie said. And she took a step, grabbed the doorknob and opened the door to the shared hallway. As she opened the door, the fern by the window trembled. "Everything, everything in this house is unstable," she said, hiking her knapsack higher on her back.

Mark put Jimbo down—back feet, front feet—and then the cat leaned into a walk toward his food bowl. His one true love.

"This house sucks, Mark," Julie said, watching Jimbo go. "It was a mistake. You were right all along." A waft of pot smoke floated in, one of the only signs of life for Tommy, their housemate. Julie never said words like fuck or suck. Generally, she found swearing untidy.

"We had an understanding," Mark said. "We said it was an open relationship. We agreed on that."

"In theory," Julie said. "We agreed in theory, Mark."

Mark considered that—the theories they agreed upon were many. He thought about the house, the cat. All the plants he'd have to water living here alone. Fuck the plants, he thought.

The day they first saw the house he had been skeptical about the whole idea of having a home, of ownership—he saw himself as a Renter with a capital R. He saw himself as Uncommitted with a capital U. "It seems a bit small, Julie," he said. "And pricey. We'd have to get a roommate to afford the mortgage. I mean …." He squinted up at the little house that did seem filled with a kind of optimism, with the sun slanting just so and the crooked tree in the small front yard. A tree that would soon strangle their sewer line with its roots, but how could they have known that?

Julie mentioned coziness, romantic togetherness. She hadn't mentioned a future, but she'd turned toward him in the afternoon light, and her black hair followed after her—glinting. She smiled. She'd thrust her arms out at her sides with a kind of Mary Tyler Moore-in-the-opening-credits flair. "My arms open this wide," she'd said. "That's all the space I need, Mark." They both knew this wasn't true, but in that moment it had seemed so possible. Her blue eyes did that lighting-up thing that was electric. A great performance.

Mark didn't mention anything about arms and their length. He worried about the roof and how long the furnace would last. But he'd hugged her that day, and in an uncharacteristic fit of abandonment, he'd put his arms out at his sides and spun like an airplane madly around the front yard. He'd spun until the front yard, the trees, and the house itself compulsed around him and then he fell like rain.

"It's perfect," he said, breathing hard. Perfect for them, even though he was lying, but he also wasn't lying.

This is how hindsight worked, he realized as he looked at Julie not smiling in the afternoon sun that crept across the room, her two suitcases sentries to a new, wonderful world she'd live in.

"You've grown," he said. It seemed like she'd gotten so tall in the last year.

Skyler Melnick

The Head Garden

Our town beheads people like there's no tomorrow. For anything, really. Petty crimes, insubordination, being in the wrong place at the wrong time. All of my family is headless. Except for me. We don't talk about it. We can't. Try speaking without a mouth and see where it gets you.

My time is coming. Don't know where, don't know when, but I feel certain my days are but a countdown, 'til government officials call me in and give me the big chop. And after they do, I'll wander off somewhere, my small, headless body searching for greener pastures. I'll walk on my hands and knees, like a cow, gnawing on the earth for sustenance, peaceful groans emanating from where my oral cavity once was.

"Run away with me," my childhood best friend, Martin, tells me. He still has his head, and is very dearly attached to it.

"Where shall we go?" I play along.

"Anywhere." He puts his hand on mine. It's clammy. "Things can't be like this everywhere. There's got to be a place that's more civilized."

"Martin." I stroke his hand. He looks at me like he's going to kiss me, so I shift my gaze to the ground. "Your head isn't all that great to begin with. Your eyes are asymmetrical. Your nose is so crooked. I feel bad about that one—I do. I never meant to hit you so hard, but now it's made you irrevocably ugly. And you can't grow facial hair for your life. I don't see what you're so upset about."

Martin doesn't speak to me for several weeks. I don't see him at school, because we stopped going months ago, in the eleventh grade, when decaptations became more frequent and less prompted.

I go to the head garden to ponder my thoughts. The heads aren't on spikes or anything gruesome like that. They're lined up on shelves, like books at a library. Check out who you please. This is where I go to confide in my mother. Shelf 177, Row E. I'll stare into her stony gray eyes—they're kept open—and tell her my troubles. But today I decide to wander, to imagine where my head will end up. Families were kept together at first, but now there's simply not enough room to be so precious about it.

I stroll through the shelves, trailing my fingers along the jaws of the heads. Prickly, prickly. The male facial hair keeps on growing.

And then I feel a familiar face. The nose I dented so many years ago, back when I was angry about everything. I look into those muddy brown eyes and decide to finally give him what he wanted all along. Our lips meet passionately—well, on my end. I part his thin flaps and trail my tongue along his teeth. The enamel's smooth, pristine. He must have brushed thoroughly before. He's like that, always prepared.

Cameron Vanderwerf

Collector

I asked the collector why he collects. He just shrugged and said, "It all increases in value."

He lived next door, and I'd go over there sometimes when Mom was at one of her jobs. He of course never let me play with anything that was still in its packaging, but he had a lot of video games. Sometimes he played *Goldeneye* with me, and he always won. Sometimes he let me play adventure games on my own, while he sat at the nearby table and worked on Gundam models with the focus of a brain surgeon.

And sometimes he let me wander the halls and rooms of his small house, inspecting his displays, looking but never touching. He'd installed shelves specifically to hold parts of his vast collection. Action figures stood, still in their boxes, in endless rows. Faces of familiar and unfamiliar characters looked back at me through plastic. I saw a first-run Han Solo figure, still in its box, and it occurred to me that he was frozen in carbonite all over again.

Glass cases held models and figurines and even some precious, autographed memorabilia. A Starfleet shirt with DeForest Kelley's signature hung in its own picture frame on a wall. "People are idiots," the collector once said, "for not getting that McCoy was always the best character."

Rows and rows of stacked boxes held his comic book collection, and sometimes he'd let me read some of the less valuable ones, as long as I wore his special pair of acid-free gloves designed for just such a purpose.

The house proper wasn't large enough to contain the entire collection, and the overflow was consigned to the basement. "The catacombs," he once called it, while clutching a bottle of beer. He let me go down there, once or twice. The place was packed with dehumidifiers to keep everything crisp and cool. "It's a bitch on the electric bill," he said, "but it's worth it." Everything stood on plastic palettes, raising all of the merchandise four inches off the ground, in case of flooding.

I didn't know how old the collector was, but looking back, I'd put his age at 40 or so. He lived alone and held down a job. I think he might have been a retail manager, but I never asked. And he never asked me about school, which was fine by me, because I didn't like fifth grade.

I never saw anyone in his house besides me and him. He never declined to let me come over. He never seemed to have other plans. When I was there, he just ignored me or didn't, according to his will, like I was some innocuous apparition that had taken up residence among his hoard. Sometimes he played board games with me, although many of them were far too complicated, featuring complex intergalactic economies, or byzantine rule sets that read like legal text books.

A few times, he sat with me on the couch and flipped through trading card albums like they were scrapbooks of family photos. I'd point to creatures that interested me, and he would explain their powers, their backstories, and their utility within the game. Once, he even gave me a card as a gift. I'd expressed admiration for its holofoil design and its depiction of a fearsome-looking dragon. "Take it, if you like it so much" he said. "I have a bunch of duplicates." I watched, wide-eyed, as he slipped it from its place in the album. Then he transferred it to a separate plastic cover and handed it to me with a casualness that seemed somehow unbefitting. I kept that card in a place of honor in my room, stuffed between old issues of Zoobooks that I hadn't read in years.

I asked him again one day, why he collects, and he gave me the same answer about the appreciation of value. But I'd never seen him sell any of it. His collection just continued to accrete, gradually but steadily. I'd show up to his house, and he'd be opening an eBay box containing vintage Pogs, or new Funko Pop figures, or an unopened, special-edition cereal that advertised a cartoon movie released twenty years ago.

I tried another tack, and I asked him, when he did finally cash it all in, what he would buy with the money. He just looked at me blankly, like I'd posed some impossible koan.

One day, Mom picked me up from the collector's house to take me to a birthday party. I didn't want to go. Jake, the birthday boy, liked to kick me in the shins and steal my glasses. But Mom liked Jake's dad, so she insisted she let her take me.

Mom arrived from the early shift at work and changed out of the clothes that the restaurant made her wear. The shirt depicted a cartoon rat leering at lasagna. When she came to the collector's house to get me, I was slashing through ninjas on an old PlayStation while the collector arranged enamel pins.

The collector invited Mom inside. He always became very friendly around her. A stark contrast from his usual bored stoicism. Mom politely declined his invitation, saying we were already late.

At the party, I sat quietly on a couch in the living room while a movie played. From the kitchen, I could hear the chatter of the adults and the hiss of drinks being opened. I peeked in during a slow part of the movie and saw Mom laughing with Jake's dad.

Mom had insisted I bring a present. I'd picked out some neon green Gak at the toy store. Jake's face twisted up when he saw the tag saying it was from me. Then he opened it and sneered. "Thanks, dipshit," he said, before letting it drop onto the carpet.

I kept asking Mom if we could leave, and she kept pretending she didn't hear me. She just continued talking to Jake's dad. Mom and I were among the last guests to leave, sometime around dusk.

After that day, Mom was gone even more often—sometimes with work, sometimes with Jake's dad—so I began spending even more time at the collector's house. He asked me about Mom a few times. "Is she seeing anyone, or .?" I didn't know what he meant, so I just shrugged.

Only a few months after Jake's birthday, Mom said that we were moving out of our apartment to live in Jake's dad's house. I asked if that meant they were getting married. She just giggled at the question, but not in an excited way. She seemed a little uncomfortable, or embarrassed.

When I told the collector that Mom and I would be moving away, he seemed sad. I wanted to believe that it was because he would miss me, but I got the feeling that that wasn't it.

The day that we moved out of the apartment, Mom loaded things into Jake's dad's big car. Jake was sitting in the back seat, scowling out at me through the window. Earlier, at his dad's command, Jake had helped carry a few things out of the apartment. He found the holofoil card the collector had given me, and he tore it into a dozen pieces.

Before we left, I went to see the collector one last time. He didn't answer when I rang his doorbell. I walked to the back and found him sitting on a plastic chair. He was drinking old collectible Ghostbusters Ecto-Coolers from the eighties. We didn't say anything. He just cracked one open and handed it to me. I took a big sip. It tasted like lime-flavored battery acid and a few fistfuls of sugar.

After a moment, I produced the dozen or so pieces of the card that Jake had torn up, and I hesitantly showed them to the collector. "Bummer," he said, looking impassively at the scraps in my palm. "That's what you might call 'no longer mint condition.'"

I closed my fingers around the pieces, then forced myself to finish the rest of the soda. I drank it so fast that it hurt. Eventually, the collector and I said our brief goodbyes.

At the new house, I rinsed out the can and let it dry before inserting the torn pieces of card into it, one by one. Then I found a hiding place under my new bed, where the collection might remain untouched for a long time.

Anna Leahy

Points of Failure

For anything of complexity,
only some things must work perfectly.
Do-overs, back-ups, safeties, alarms—
there are ways to cover your ass.
If you give each point of potential
failure enough attention, you'll know
what to do, you'll know not to do it.
Still, you'll collapse comets
and women as they give way.

> My *so thin* blurted to the bride I
> hardly know and know better than
> to say. To a mother, something about
> boys with an assumption, a disinclination
> I see as I say it. Apologies unsaid
> because *sorry* is a tether to missing evidence
> of good intentions. Even when the bee
> leaves, the stinger works barbs into skin.
> Venom takes seconds I waste and want.

Everything's a three-body problem:
head, thorax, abdomen || sun, earth, eye.
The idea is to keep, to hold
positions relative, to unfold
wings as if they are breath and a web

of golden mirrors. What else
might we see with mosaic eyes
and hexagon reflections in worlds
of unstable equilibrium?

From Earth, we'll have the ability see
a honeybee alight on the moon
if only a honeybee were there
with everything that I want to unsay.

—*after Sylvia Plath and the James Webb Tele-
scope*

Matthew Guenette

Domesticity

… pour honey over a sex toy then plant it gently in an anthill. Keep feeling fascination just like the song. Start a punk band with a bunch of fifty-somethings called The Richard Marxists or Unattached Sentient Jell-O or Dirty Nightie or The Well Hungarians or Tammy Faye Bakker's Dozen, etc. Work on your back and hips, then eat oatmeal for a week. Stand at a busy intersection in a sandwich board that reads: *HAVE YOU SEEN ME?* Wear a hazmat suit to an academic conference. Hug the oldest tree you can find, I mean really hug it, unironically, like you're horny in love. Write a novel where every chapter begins with an unnamed narrator trying to cancel a credit a credit card and ends with the credit card extremely uncanceled. Stay sober; see how it feels. Stack a cord of wood with a friend. Talk politics with a chimney sweep. Start a food cart called *Full of Schnitzel* with menu items like "Bull Schnitzel" and "Eat Schnitzel and Die." Do you really not know what you want? Are you afraid if you say it your small corner of the world will explode? What if we just tell each other exactly how we feel? I'll go first: *Sometimes I want you all to myself.*

Rich Glinnen

Planet Fitness

I was at the gym, trying to use the triceps machine
in a way that didn't make my elbows click,
when I overheard one of the staff members speaking to a mechanic
who was dismantling the machine beside me.

The staff member was saying there was a problem
with the chest press machine in the other room—
the pin was stuck in the stack of weighted plates.
She tried removing it, she said, but it's *really stuck*.

I know what she's talking about,
because I, too, tried removing that pin just the other day
when it was chest day. It didn't budge, so I gave up
and used the machine next to it,
where my flabby chest and I
observed a sweaty stream of unworthy men
get turned away by the stubborn piece of steel.

But I have faith in this man, for he is a mechanic,
a sorcerer of tools, who has ridden to this strip mall
in his tall white horse of a van
to rescue our plummeting pectorals,

a mere pair of Nathan's hot dogs
giving him the power to free Excalibur from the stone,
to rule over us all, his planet of kneeling subjects,
whose sea of clicking knees shower
our judgment-free king with undying loyalty.

Sally Ashton

July, How Far I Fly

Yes, there were hundreds of satellites to keep track of. Yes, a jet rumbled on its course from time to time, but clocks on Earth had begun to follow a curious logic, so who knew. They called it a Metal Rat Year. I never found out what that meant, but it sounded right. Somewhere deep in the house, footsteps could be heard crossing, recrossing the hardwood. Somewhere a dog barked. It seemed endless. I turned the page; nothing lasts forever. Something about the law of nature, something about the dream of man. A fine-tuned car alarm blasted one note for several uninterrupted minutes, then silence. Nothing lasts. Turn the page. Turn the page, which was how I sometimes read the world. Pretty much everything in space spins, and now I felt it at the quantum level. How long could I hold my breath? July clear, hot, with a chance of sorrow, but honey, that was just life in the late Anthropocene.

Lauren D. Woods

Timetable for Learning to Eat Alone

One week: The time after which you may wish to dispose of any spices, condiments, or other edibles the two of you shared together. Condiments, though a delight to the taste buds, may, after all, only distract from a deeper need to nourish and satiate.

One month: The period of time after which you will begin to try dessert again, a slice of pie, perhaps, without your tongue sticking to the roof of your mouth. A recipe, like one for pie, may be passed down for generations, and if it is an old one, like your grandmother's pecan pie recipe, which reminds you of the pecan trees outside her Fort Worth home that stretched up high arms and littered the yard with heavy pecans that you then scooped up as a child into paper bags and shared with your grandmother, it is good to be cautious with the recipe, because recipes also contain instructions for dishes that represent acts of familial love, repeated over generations.

Two months: The length of time during which you will carefully curl your thumb under while cutting—a technique your mother taught you to stay safe, which you carelessly disregarded, because your mind was elsewhere, because something felt off, causing you to slice open your thumb while chopping nuts, before he bandaged your thumb gently with a cheese cloth.

Three months: The length of time during which you will periodically shudder in front of the gas burner.

Four months: The time it will take for you to use a knife and cutting board without feeling phantom arms around you; also, incidentally, the average number of months couples report it takes to fall in love. Falling out is another timetable entirely.

Five months: The time it takes before you begin to appreciate your own kitchen enough to cut out a page from a book of poetry, something by David Whyte, with the line that says, *The kettle is singing even as it pours you a drink*, and hang it to the left of your stove. After that, you will fill your window with aloe and thyme and parsley and gaze over the pots, outside to the courtyard below, while something simmers behind you, and breathe in a quiet, solitary evening.

Six months: The time it takes before you can find the right combination of cinnamon, nutmeg, and clove to approximate the smell of a cozy home. Cinnamon is native to Sri Lanka; ancient Egyptians used it in embalming, and the Roman Emperor Nero ordered a year's supply to be burned after he murdered his wife. In the sixteen and seventeen hundreds, various European countries fought each other over access to the spice. In modern times, particularly in winter, the scent of cinnamon may be used as a substitute for the elusive feeling of romantic and familial love.

Seven months: The length of time it will take to sip green tea without feeling a tingle down your spine, the way you did when he slipped outside for phone calls while you heated the kettle. The phone calls usually went on quietly, with him smoking a cigarette, pacing, and once, when you stepped out to take out the trash, you thought you may have caught the particular pitch of a woman's voice on the other end.

Eight months: The time it takes to drive by the house you moved into together, complete with the renovated kitchen and gas burners, without feeling your stomach drop. Incidentally, the layout reminded you of one particular summer dinner from your childhood, with your mother sharing a chicken-and-rice dish, your father pouring honey onto white dinner rolls, and the gentle rolling of your contented stomach as you savored the last bites.

Nine months: The time it takes before you experience the quiet satisfaction of a vegetarian noodle recipe chosen by you, with ripe squash and tomatoes that give just so—a meal made with care by one and for one only. This meal will far surpass any of the others, and years later, you will remember with wonder the aroma, the sizzling skillet, careful cuts made with skill by your own hands, with tenderness.

Ten months: The length of time it will take for you to finally pull out the cheese tray you carefully arranged for your guests the night you happened to come upon him kissing another woman, and slipping away with her, alone, into the kitchen next to a pie warming on a gas stovetop. Incidentally, earlier the same evening, a knife slipped carelessly from your hand, while chopping nuts, onto your own thumb. You could not help but hear, in this instance, the tenor of the other voice, and find it similar to the one you thought might have been coming through the receiver in those quiet evening calls.

Eleven months: The length of time it takes to make another pecan pie like the one you made that night, when he wrapped his arms around you and said, "Careful, you're going to make me marry you." It would not be the memory of the pie, much later, that would make you shudder in front of the gas burner, but the other part. Food, after all, is transitory, passing quickly through your digestive system, except of course, for those portions that remain with you and become part of the fabric of your cells.

Twelve months: The time it takes for a cheese tray or a knife to lose their significance. Utensils, after all, are merely tools for cooking. Recipes, though passed down through generations, are merely suggestions for repeated nourishment over time, and only gain their significance when served with true affection. This is the time it takes, more or less, for an old pie spatula to settle in the back of a drawer and become nothing more than metal triangle attached to a black wooden cylinder, slicing through a gooey mess that too is nothing more substantive than a sweet, empty concoction of calories.

J. Haase Vetter

Going Before the Board

We'll come to order. The first case on our agenda this morning is regarding Jenn Vetter and her current life choices. Are all parties present and ready?

Good. Now, our records show that at 8 p.m. Pacific time on Tuesday, January 20, Ms. Vetter, the defendant, said the following: "Tomorrow I'm going to get so much done." Are our records correct, Ms. Vetter?

Yes, your honor.

Alright then. Our records also show that on Wednesday, January 21, you rose at 7:30, a full hour after your husband. Is this correct?

Yes, your honor. On the days I don't work, I try to get more sleep.

You then proceed to put on the same yoga pants you've worn for the last eight days and the sweatshirt you've worn for ... that can't be right ... this sweatshirt has had the same toothpaste mark on the cuff for the past thirty-eight days. Ms. Vetter, you do know that toothpaste will come out in the wash. Right?

Yes, your honor.

You spend twelve minutes at the kitchen table with your children and then proceed to move to the couch. You then pick up *The Stone Sky*, read three pages and trade the book for your phone. After that, you play the free games on *The New York Times* website and then open something on your phone called ... *Gardenscapes*? Ms. Vetter, what is *Gardenscapes*?

Well, umm. There's a butler and a garden, and in order to keep adding to your garden, you need to win this matching game.

I see. And you're on level 759?

That seems possible.

At 8:30, you rise from the couch to change into your "outside pants," put shoes and coat on, and walk your children to school. You return at 9:15, change back into your yoga pants and return to the couch. Does all of this seem correct?

Yes, your honor.

Again, there is *Gardenscapes* with the addition of scrolling through Facebook and Instagram. I see you stopped several times over ads purporting to help you in your art career. The phone is put down at … really, Ms. Vetter … 10:05?

Yes, I believe I was getting tired of sitting.

Imagine. You then wander around the house for about five minutes. You consume a slice of cheese and pet your cat, Borte.

She's named for Ghengis Khan's first wife.

Cute. Oh, this is promising; at 10:20, you turn on the computer and check your email. At 10:23, you open the document entitled "Bullies," and you spend fifteen minutes editing.

Yes, that's one of my stories.

You then spend the next twenty-five minutes submitting the document, presumably for publication?

Yes, that's correct.

And now we're back on *Gardenscapes*. Ms. Vetter, it's now a little after 11 a.m., and I'm wondering when you're going to "get stuff done"?

OK, I know it looks bad, but it's still early. I don't go to bed until ten, so there's still time.

All right, let's see where we go from here. There's a brief break for lunch, you've heated up some leftovers, and then you sit down to do work for your actual job. This is nice. I see you have a clipboard with some kind of accounting system for your students' work. Excellent. You work for approximately thirty-six minutes. And then what's happening here?

I think I'm listening to a podcast.

You appear to be looking out the window.

I'm thinking about going outside since it's finally stopped raining.

For twenty minutes?

I guess so.

You guess so. OK, you then leave the house! Well, this is interesting. Where did you go?

To buy chicken feed.

And then you fed the chickens. OK, we'll give you a point for that. You read for a half-hour and then leave to pick up your children from school. You've had six hours without responsibility, and our calculations say you spent approximately ninety minutes on "getting stuff done."

Ms. Vetter, the panel is having a hard time understanding why you should be allowed this much free time, as you are clearly unable to use it wisely.

Yes, your honor.

Given your particular circumstances, we sentence you to minor stomach cramps and insomnia until you get your act together. If that is not motivation enough, we will have to resort to more drastic measures.

Please, No.

That's right, if you cannot manage to at least set some goals and make an effort, we will have to give you gas and constipation. You will find that the only remedy for those pains will involve intense aerobic exercise.

And please, Ms. Vetter, for goodness sake, can you sit up straight for once? Your core strength is not on trial, but that may be next.

Suphil Lee Park

Hap

합(合)/*hap/: the Korean notion that a union
of two or more compatibles brings forth a great
synergy, may they be food ingredients or people,
because everything has opposing or synergizing
counterparts*

The amount of sugar it takes to make jam is a sure health hazard even at a glance. But the subdued, lazy sizzle of fruits softening and soaking up all that sugar works like a white noise machine, only it brings you to a more awake lull. Yezi's compact kitchen, something that seems whipped up begrudgingly as an afterthought, is littered with peaches of all varieties, from nectarine to saturn. Her kitchen looks out onto a bleak Brooklyn street through a stubborn hopper window, but Yezi has her back turned on the street view now, occupied. She busies her hands with the peaches she dropped earlier on her way home, massaging each one with flour to get the dirt off before gently cleansing it under running water. Then she pries the peach apart using her fingers and pulls the pit out. For a while, she becomes lost in the offbeat tune of the peach pits clanging into the bowl and the crooning pot of jam in the making, her hands mindlessly working. The saturn peaches are ripe with red specks, which her Korean mother would have called "taste buds," or *miroe*.

Her roommate-slash-cameraman, Ethan, mouths words opposite her, pointing at the ASMR recording device set beside the stove. *Almost done*, Yezi gestures back and returns to pitting the last few peaches and adding them to the piles. Before turning off the recorder, Yezi takes out mason jars, each labeled with the name of a different peach variety. *So much of life is spent on sorting*, her mother once said, briefly cupping a Fuji in one palm before declaring it extra fancy. Around her, three acres of peach and pear and apple trees. So much of life does go into sorting and understanding the criteria, Yezi thinks. Years into months, anniversaries, events. Cities into different boroughs. People into acquaintances, friends, neighbors, blunders, lovers. Fruits into jam, marmalade, jelly, or coulis. Sometimes the difference is minimal, so nuanced that it leads to discord on the criteria themselves. And the sheer audacity to think, nevertheless, the differences will surely be understood. Yezi turns off the recorder and sits beside Ethan, who plays the recording for the pre-editing review before they can decide when or whether to upload the video to her staggering YouTube channel.

Their Brooklyn apartment, apart from its bemusingly angled layout, is not that different from the one she'd rented in a provincial Korean college town for the better half of her twenties. Back then, her studio's poorly ventilated kitchen had been fed so much grease and smoke over the years, so many nutrients for life, whenever she waited for water to boil, she could feel its thin walls breathing like another layer of her skin. Its only window, the size of an extra-small crop top, displayed a fragment of the old oak tree in front of the apartment building in dim streetlights. The oak's branches looked as if they had been stolen from another species and welded on at random but spooked her no more by the time she had to bicker with the landlord over utility bills for the fourth time. And by the time she decided to leave the apartment, and the country altogether, all of her life savings in American stocks, she walked around, fished a towel from the rack, retrieved cooking utensils, unplugged her cell phone charger, and did everything in her apartment with the thoughtless confidence of familiarity. *Something more*, she thought one night, with the kind of optimism that stems only from young desperation. Or perhaps, if she had a moment to reflect and articulate: *anything new.*

The recording starts: "Hello, everyone. Today I'm going to make jam with five different peach varieties, then sample and review each of them." Each word whispered but enunciated. Yezi in the video, hidden out of the camera angle from above her lips, summarizes the function of ASMR and its tingling, soothing effects on the insomniacs and recommends that viewers put their earphones in and turn up the volume. The video then zooms out on the five heaps of pitted, halved peaches, followed by peaches softly thumping against each other in rustling brown bags. That harmony reminds Yezi of a late summer in her early girlhood. Her tutu thrown on the floor in haste, sweaty from an hour of barre work, she'd drink chilled barley tea right out of its bottle in big gulps, the fridge door open. After all the bustling noises of tulles and frantic little pointe shoes, she'd revel in that thirst that drowns out everything else, without even knowing what reveling meant. Then she'd hungrily turn to something, anything, to eat, in the empty apartment and usually settle on steamed corn from the night before. When she casually talked about this with Ethan one time, eyes foggy with nostalgia, he cut her short by asking, in disbelief, "You were nine and just walked back and forth to your ballet practice alone?" And she stared back at him blankly, still not understanding.

The video now closes up on Yezi's hands rhythmically pulling apart one peach after another. She pauses the video there and turns to Ethan. "What do you think?"

"This is gonna make tens of thousands drop asleep, I'd say, just two minutes in," he throws a deadpan joke. "I'd add some of your farming anecdotes, just to make sure that hardcore insomniacs are also taken care of."

They banter a little more but fall quickly silent as Ethan resumes the video. Yezi savors the lemon zest in her coffee he bought from the corner coffee shop while Ethan watches the rest. Another, unexpected flavor, a faintest hint of cinnamon, makes her want to ask: Do you know, instead of spicing up hot drinks or bakeries, Koreans use cinnamon to make a traditional punch? But then she'd have to go on. How the essence of cinnamon is warmth. How that essence alleviates the harmful effects of a cold punch. How the culinary traditions of her country have evolved upon a single idea: Everything in nature has an essential element that complements, cancels out, or contradicts another. A mispairing of two independently harmless ingredients can turn out detrimental, or even lethal. Ethan once said: Instead of starting off with *Do you know*, you should just say, *I know you don't know but I know*.

But most of the time, Yezi doesn't know if Ethan, or anyone, shares her point of view that all those tidbits of her odd, increasingly foreign knowledge accumulate to form a world like a web of neurons firing and misfiring. Elements clashing. Strangers coming into contact to enliven, brush past, or hurt one another.

Yezi stands up and steps over to the side of the kitchen where she left a few envelopes open. She elbows them aside to the edge of the jutting windowsill—the way she would push aside the thoughts that keep her up late into the night. Next content for her channel to placate the miserable insomniacs surfing for a white noise machine alternative, her expiring visa, postcards from her gradually more distant old friends in Korea, the ones who took to backpacking across Europe between jobs, the creases Ethan left on her pillow, or her old life not so different from the one now, out of context, all that she left behind or thought she had. America seems never short of people who left. Especially in New York. Especially in Korea Town, where Yezi's been working between classes, although it also seems stuck in a culture and a time period everyone was supposed to have left behind. On break, Yezi would often find herself surrounded by a group of girls with frizzy tassels of dyed hair, ESL students on lunch break, exchange students sallow from barhopping, visibly homesick honeymooners (what kind of people *choose* to honeymoon in NYC, she always wondered), draft dodgers, hairstylist trainees nursing their chaffed, nicked fingers, compatriots of all kinds who departed from the very peninsula she'd left, only to be stranded, in transition, or moderately thriving. She'd always feel invisible and singled out at the same time in that strange street, far from any figurative or real "town," at the waist of Manhattan. *But no matter*, she'd always brush it off. That's what one ought to learn—she'd decided a few months into her new life, that when passing through a constantly crumbling, shifting world, there's just much to brush off.

Yezi takes a bite out of one of the halved peaches. The tart pulp effortlessly gives under her teeth, the way it's supposed to, just right for the jam. But without looking, she'd also believe it to be any variety she's told it is.

Matthias Politycki

Fever Fantasy (I)

Sick in a foreign country.
Chambermaids
always come again
to put a dry sheet on your bed.

One smiles
only fleetingly.
The other lays
her hand on your forehead
and shakes her head.

With one you will
almost immediately recover.
With the other you are already
as good as dead.

Translated from the German by Brendan Stephens

Matthias Politycki

Fever Fantasy (II)

Left behind in a yurt
on the edge of the Kazakh steppe,
you lie ill in your camp
and listen to the chorale of the sheep
in the evening, then hear a drum
and throaty song,
the clapping of the audience,
the cheers of dancers,
at the end of the festival, music still
plays from a car radio. Hours later
you hear the snort of a horse,
the squeak of a camel.
Then it really begins,
the great steppe silence.
Until dawn, you listen
only to the wind as it drives through grasses.
And many little shrieks,
sometimes a squeak or a rattle,
then there's dying out there.

If you survive the night,
at the first cockcrow
everything starts over again.

Translated from the German by Brendan Stephens

SM Stubbs

Asylum Early Days

That first night, the sky was a glittering riverbed,
      the shape of the life to come, the mood almost

a party, streamers, punch and music in the halls.
      Lying awake, questions: What good is a balloon?

Leave it alone, it vanishes, an ever-fading suggestion
      of joy. He can't stand this stereo punctuation, this

fever of sound, the shivering funhouse of things
      he isn't. Only allowed the book of miracles he

may not forge the nails but he knows what they do.
      Pierce the flesh! Yes. *Connect the dots.* Yes. *Join the wood*

that holds up the body that holds up the world. His neighbor
      says a fog's settling in, people so hazy and urgent

in their needs. His eyes cannot drink you fast enough,
      thirst unquenchable. He's in trouble with his god

and the meaning of love's coded into the scripture.
      He's wondering whose bones he'll fall asleep on.

SM Stubbs

Asylum Pests

Now bees in the walls. Probably. At night
　　　I nod into sleep while the TV warbles. I hear

plaster fall and knock against the beams
　　　behind the bricks and that begs a causation,

this followed by that. The way California
　　　shakes when tectonic plates collide. The way

a single spark ruins whatever wants to burn.
　　　I see stories about people finding huge nests

in the walls of their houses, under the eaves.
　　　In biology class we grew colonies of fruit flies

to learn the best ways for them to die: vinegar
　　　and a drop of soap. I want to wake in a world

where nothing asks to test me, where people
　　　behave in ways I can ignore without crying.

What's in the walls gets closer. I look forward
　　　to the day someone sets this place on fire.

Kate Gehan

Lucky

The dead grandmothers want you to send up a flare when you're in need. Sob them every hormonal song from your electric, changeling body. *Zap za-zing!* Don't bother with deep breathing, sweetheart! Ruin something as a signal. Burn the crust of the key lime pie or fall asleep in a hammock instead of consoling a distraught man and they'll show up wild—leopard-print miniskirts, camisoles, unkempt hair long and dyed turquoise—no pantyhose or flat-ironed blond bobs for these dames. The dead grandmothers are fully in love with themselves because it's high time. They have each other now. They have themselves. They don't care where the grandfathers have gone. They're interested in cheesecake and a French 75.

If you're fourteen they'll snuggle up on the sectional beside you and watch trash television, blush at the ponytailed men with burly arms on dating shows, *tsk tsk* over your high school crush who can't match his socks, let alone text you back. The dead grandmothers will throw 4 a.m. dance parties and tattoo you on the bathroom floor. If you're forty-eight, they'll peer in the bathroom vanity and tell you to stop worrying about smile lines. Honey, get a younger lover and book a Caribbean trip. Turn your face towards the heat.

While you sleep the dead grandmothers meet themselves in the forest and flirt, slip themselves free. They don't waste time sucking up car exhaust at Newark airport waiting for a late lover. They don't fold themselves into silver sedans to kiss men through a cloud of cologne and Winston smoke anymore. They don't even need patience, and one day you'll understand irrelevance, too. The dead grandmothers slide and soak into the fragrant night to take flight on the backs of insects whose names you can't be bothered to learn.

DS Levy

Walk-Through

*If you don't break your ropes while you're alive
do you think
ghosts will do it after?*

—*Kabir*

Halfway down the hallway, Babette feels a tap on her shoulder, turns around and sees a long-haired ghost, a big effervescent gal with translucent arms adamantly crossed over her chest. "Fair warning," the ghost whispers. "I come with the house."

"I'll keep that in mind," Babette says, catching up to her husband, who's close enough to grab the Realtor's ass and conga dance into the master-on-the-main.

The Realtor, Jasmine, is dressed casual-chic: slinky tank top, jeans tight as second skin, black-and-white polka-dot kitten heels. Tim found her business card, with her glamour headshot, in a coffee shop and scheduled the viewing even though he knew Babette had no intention of moving.

Another tap.

"Hey, I thought you'd be afraid of me."

"Sorry to disappoint."

The bedroom has a beautiful fireplace made of pudding stone which, Jasmine says, was shipped downstate from Drummond Island.

"Nice." Tim touches the smooth stones, firm, like Jasmine's breasts. "Real nice."

"I'm telling ya, that guy's trouble." The ghost swirls over Babette's shoulder. "My name's Xenyon, by the way. Don't ask—my mom was a hippie."

Babette taps a structural wall: solid. "And you're haunting this place because?"

"I was coming out of the shower and *Bang*!" Xenyon points at her chest. "Only meant to scare me, he said. My husband always did have a lousy aim."

"He shot you?" Babette gasps, looks around for signs of blood, blown-off bits of skin, and accidentally knocks over a standing towel rack.

"You break it, you buy it," Tim jokes from the bedroom.

Xenyon mimics holding a gun to her head, pretending to fire, her head recoiling from the blast. "He got twenty-five years. If he doesn't get out early on good behavior."

"Wow, your own husband," Babette says, unaware that across the hallway, Tim ducks into a closet.

"Wow is right." The ghost fluffs her hair. "And I'm stuck in this fucking house, bored out of my mind!"

Jasmine and Tim step out of the closet, giggling. His libidinous eyes blink a warning: *fair game*. Jasmine pouts her lips and swaggers like a pole dancer—which, Babette knows, wouldn't be the first dancer Tim's romanced.

They go upstairs, Babette huffing and puffing, trying to keep up. She keeps meaning to go back to the gym and lose some weight. She keeps meaning to do a lot of things.

"How many?" Xenyon asks.

"Steps?" Babette takes a deep breath.

"No, lovers."

"Truthfully, lost count."

"Damn. That's cold."

Jasmine and Tim move down the hallway—a beige Berber that's seen better days. Babette peeks into a bedroom—roomy and light—but no Jasmine, no Tim. She checks out the room across the hall—desk, computer, printer—and catches her husband running his finger down Jasmine's sculpted arm.

"And this is the office," Jasmine says, pulling back as Babette steps into the room. "Or another bedroom, if you prefer."

"I'm telling you," Xenyon whispers. "I've seen this shit-show before. Ever watched 'The Cuckqueans of 90512'?"

"I love that show!" Babette giggles and reaches out to touch Xenyon's shoulder, but her fingers slice through the whispery form.

Following Jasmine through the doorway, Tim whispers, "Babs, you're fucking talking to yourself again."

The basement has "a lovely walkout with theater and full bar," Babette hears the Realtor coo. She lags behind, stopping in the chilly kitchen. On top of the counter, one leg draped over the other, is gum-popping Xenyon.

"You know," Xenyon says, "I could really help you."

Through her shimmering body, Babette notices a decorative plaque on the wall—it, too, is all wrong, too retro. "How?"

"I'll spook the shit outta him, move things around, make noises." Xenyon makes a hissing sound like the wind. "Better yet—." A ceramic bowl impressively levitates in midair.

In the basement, no doors open or close. There's no chat about the theater system. Then: giggles, throaty rebuffs, purring seduction.

Xenyon frowns. "Well?"

Babette looks around; too much dark wood, brassy knobs, fluorescent light. And the countertop—olive green laminate!

"Hmm," she says, thinking. "There's so much that needs updating."

Xenyon beams. "C'mon, let's have some fun!"

Babette studies the stodgy white walls, the seventies light fixtures, the crown molding and single-hung windows. She thinks about Jasmine's promise: that their current home—modern, comfortable, stylish—the one Babette has always assumed she'd live in happily-ever-after, will sell in a heartbeat.

Xenyon winks, pops her pink bubble gum. It's been years since Babette has had a real friend, one she doesn't have to worry about becoming Tim's next conquest.

On the stairs, footsteps. On the top step, Jasmine adjusts her silk blouse.

Xenyon shakes her tremulous head in disgust.

"You haven't checked out the basement yet," Tim says.

"I've seen enough," Babette says, winking at Xenyon. For the first time in a long time, there's an eerie light at the end of the tunnel. "I say we make an offer—one they can't refuse."

Susan Holcomb

Bad Math

I come from a family of entrepreneurs. My grandfather was an oil man, back in those days when, according to him, any Texan with enough gumption and a passing knowledge of geology could strike black gold. My father was in manufacturing. The product never mattered. Belts, tools, handbags—they all boiled down to the same accounting. When I was five years old, my father took me to Costco to show me the wrenches he sold. I remember walking through the giant warehouse space, where the shelves stretched up so high I couldn't see the tops of them, where the boxes of cereal and jars of margarine were packaged for bulk sale and blown up to five times their usual size. It wasn't like any store I had ever been to with my mother: It was a store for giants. My father led me to the home improvement aisle, and from the shelf he plucked a straight-jaw wrench with a rubber-coated handle. One of *ours*, he said. He handed it to me. "What do you think, Janie?" The wrench was heavier than I expected. When I dropped it to the floor, the sound echoed down the aisle.

After that I watched each episode of *Mister Rogers' Neighborhood* very carefully. Every afternoon, Mister Rogers led his viewers to a magic picture frame that transported us to the places where things were made. He took us to the kinds of family-owned American factories that exist, I now believe, only in the imaginations of certain politicians. In these factories, machines pumped out cascades of crayons, mountains of macaroni, perfectly cut rafts of construction paper. I knew these factories were not my father's. I knew he made belts and tools and handbags, not crayons or macaroni or construction paper. But every afternoon I watched and waited. Maybe today Mister Rogers would show us how they made jaw wrenches. Maybe today I would see my dad on TV.

In the years since the financial crisis, I have found myself looking with anticipation at TV screens again. I keep expecting that somewhere in the background—in the crowd behind the morning news anchors or among the detectives casing a made-up crime scene—I will see my father. There is no logic to my looking: I anticipate my father's imminent appearance on prime-time sitcoms with canned laugh tracks, on reality shows about rich women having arguments, on nature documentaries where lions hunt antelopes on the open plains. Any scene on any show can trigger my impulse to start looking, even though I know that since the recession, my father has done nothing worth recording on TV. But day after day I scan the screen for his Coke-bottle glasses, his famous checkered shirts, the mustache he hasn't had since I was a child. Not finding him, I usually flip the TV off, and on the blank screen my own reflection shines back at me.

I remember the 2008 recession as if it were a magic trick: Someone pulled the wrong ace from a deck of cards, and all at once the world changed. I had just started my second year of graduate school in the physics department of an East Coast university. I worked on the top floor of the physics building, down at the end in the theory wing. The theorists all had hilariously tiny offices, made smaller by the abundance of papers that seemed to take over every flat surface as if it were a principle of physical law: A surface once covered must stay covered, the clutter-law of inertia. My supervising professor—a young theorist who was happy to have me there to handle the grueling longhand calculations that were beneath his attention—said it would be all right for me to set up shop in the office of a professor emeritus who had recently died. Someone had taken away all of the dead professor's books, but his papers still filled the filing cabinets and covered the desk. The young theorist had me tape a handmade sign over the dead professor's nameplate on the door. *Jane Fields*, I wrote in Sharpie. *Graduate Research Fellow*.

Mid-September is the best time of year for any university: still early in the semester, the hallways all keyed up with hopeful energy. The undergraduates I taught were still showing up on time with their pencils sharpened, writing carefully in notebooks that would soon diminish both in number and in neatness as the classes thinned out from the students who gave up or simply overslept. Early that

Monday I stopped into the faculty lounge on my way to the dead professor's office. A copy of *The New York Times* was sitting abandoned by the coffee machine. I picked the paper up and read the headlines: Lehman Brothers, apparently, had gone bankrupt. I didn't really know what Lehman Brothers did, but I knew that I had heard of them, and that bankruptcy meant seriously bad news. The company had run into a problem of "leverage," the newspaper explained, exacerbated by the presence of "complex derivatives." I read that sentence over and over. I knew what a derivative was, but I couldn't reason out how calculus could crash a company. I touched my thumb to my right pinky finger, which was calloused at the knuckle from the way I wrote out my calculations, and thought of all the complicated math that populated my own notebooks. To the untrained eye, my loosely scribbled lines of squiggly Greek symbols might have looked like spells. Reading and re-reading the phrase *complex derivates*, I started to feel that the Lehman incident had confirmed what I had perhaps always expected: that too much calculating really could invoke something, and math itself could rip the fabric of the universe.

When the young professor arrived, I accosted him by the coffee machine. I had the newspaper hanging uselessly in my hand. "Have you heard about all this?" I asked. "With Lehman Brothers?"

He poured too much cream into his cup. "Wall Street, right?"

"They're saying the company's gone bankrupt."

"Wow."

I stood there while he stirred his coffee, slipped his spoon into the little sink. "Have you ever heard of a complex derivative?"

"You mean like calculus?"

"I think it's a financial term."

"Can't say I know much about finance," the young professor said. He coughed. "Speaking of. How are your calculations coming?"

My father called me that afternoon. "Lehman," he said, pronouncing it the correct way. *Lee-mun.* "This is bad news, Janie, very bad news."

I told him what I'd read about the derivatives. "They're saying the problem was bad math."

My father laughed. "It's never the math, honey—bad or otherwise. These guys knew exactly what they were doing."

"What guys? Lehman Brothers?" *Lee-mun.* I pronounced it the correct way. "You think they meant to go bankrupt?"

"Well, probably not. They may not have thought it would ever catch up to them. Whatever it was they did."

The young professor and I were just children, I thought. Out in the real world, the real adults were deciding things, doing things, making the kinds of mistakes that toppled empires. My father was saying something about the price of copper. "Look it up in *The Wall Street Journal!* In March, copper was at an all-time high. Now it's plummeting!"

I didn't understand him. "Is that bad?"

"Janie," he said, "we're in for a very rough year."

I understood this *we* to be a global one: a *we* that did not necessarily include either my father or me in particular. *We* might mean the United States of America, or the economy in the abstract, or even the world. It could not, in any sense, mean *we, us, you and me, Janie.* In the dead professor's office, my father's voice rising and falling on the telephone, I imagined myself an island.

The next week Barack Obama was set to debate John McCain. I was struggling to put together a dresser I had purchased from IKEA. The instructions showed a smiling little man sticking slats of wood together with plastic screws. I dragged the dresser drawers into the living room where I could watch the debate on TV.

On TV John McCain was saying, "The fundamentals of our economy are strong." I turned the word over in my mind: *fundamentals.* What was fundamental to an economic system? People spent money and earned money—that part was simple. So where did the *complex derivative* come in? I thought of the students in my teaching section who would no doubt drop the class that fall. *I just don't get it,* they would say. *This stuff is all over my head.* As McCain passed the microphone to Obama, I thought, *Over my head, too.*

The phone rang and I yanked my hand back from the dresser. A splinter of wood caught under my nail. I put the phone on speaker and went to search for tweezers. "Hello?"

"Jane? What are you doing?"

"I put you on speaker, Mom."

"It sounds like you're on an airplane."

"I'm home." I took the tweezers from a drawer and dug them under my nail.

"Have you spoken with your father?"

I said I had.

"How did he seem to you?" My parents had been divorced for years.

"Fine." I pulled the splinter out. "I mean—what do you mean?"

"He left me a voicemail. He was talking about money. I think he thinks he can convince me to give up some of my alimony."

"Hm."

"So I just wanted to know if he'd said anything to you."

I yanked the splinter out. Under my nail a little red spot of blood appeared. "He only called to tell me about the market crash."

"It's a bad time for business," my mother said.

Symmetry works like this: If you swap the charge of every elementary particle, negative for positive and positive for negative, the laws of physics stay the same. If you swap every particle with its mirror image, left for right and right for left, the laws of physics again stay the same. Symmetry also holds if you reverse the arrow of time. If you make the future the past and the past the future, the laws of physics stay the same. From a microscopic perspective, dropping an egg off the top of a building is the same as a broken egg reconstructing its shattered shell and flying back into your careless hand. Every day I went up to the dead professor's office and spent hours working through these time-reversal calculations: writing out matrices, solving for eigenvalues. As I worked I shifted my mental scope to the space of mathematics, my frame of reference expanding and contracting with each pencil stroke. I could pass hours like that without even noticing it; time seemed to contract itself around my calculating such that full days shrank down readily to minutes. At night I dreamed of eggs falling off of buildings and flying back up from the pavement, their shells breaking and then repairing, the yolk seeping out and sucking straight back in. Physicists love to imagine dropping things off skyscrapers, from heights so great even a falling penny could kill a pedestrian down below. In the dead professor's office, the length of my right hand gray and shiny from pencil smears, I thought of Lehman Brothers. *Lee-mun.* They must have worked out of a skyscraper in New York. The physics building where I sat was only four stories high. Our pennies, cast down from the theory wing, would neither kill nor maim.

Through all that fall my father, on the phone, spoke like a man newly converted. His voice held an edge of frantic energy that made me anxious. He would call and tell me to read this or that article in this or that newspaper. More information was coming out, something about the housing market. The newspapers, he assured me, would explain everything. The more I read, the less I understood. *I am smart,* I wanted to tell my father, *but not in this way.* What the papers said was muddled and opaque, with terms from mathematics sprinkled through like sorcery. *Sub-prime. Adjustable-rate. Derivative.* Math was supposed to make things clearer, to take the chaos of the world and make it comprehensible. But the financiers who spoke on record in the papers seemed to use math not to clarify, but to obfuscate. The more they mentioned *complex derivatives*, the less I sensed I could guess what the term might mean. When I talked to my undergraduates about quantum mechanics, they were mystified: It didn't seem real to them. But quantum mechanics was real. Supersymmetry was real. Such theories could be explained, step by step, with a pencil and paper and clear-headed thinking. What the newspapers spoke about—the market bubbles, the corporate bankruptcies, the price of copper moving up and down so that it seemed less like a tangible commodity than a divining rod—those were the things that were truly unbelievable and unexplained. "Just tell me," I said to my father one day in October, "why does the price of copper seem to matter so much?"

"It's a heuristic," he said. "A measure of volatility."

I let a beat pass. I swallowed hard. "And what is volatility?"

"It's a measure of risk, Janie."

I put my head down on the desk and set the phone beside me. The copper measured volatility, which measured risk, which meant what? How was it possible that all those people at Lehman Brothers had understood what I could not? *Lee-mun,* I thought. Perhaps they hadn't understood. Maybe all they saw were measures on measures, too. Maybe that had been the problem.

"Janie?" my father was saying. "Are you still there?"

"I'm here," I croaked, my head still on the desk. "I'm here."

I sat up and asked my father how his life was going. "The businesses," I said. "They're doing all right?"

"It has been busy," he said. "Very busy."

"And the house?"

"Oh, this damn house," he said like always. "I've got to get it cleaned up."

My father lived in a little two-story townhouse that he used to rent out to tenants before my parents divorced. In the years since my grandfather died, the place had grown hopelessly cluttered with my grandfather's things. Fine china and silver serving platters lay stacked up in armchairs. Antique vases protruded along the cramped hallway, their sides growing increasingly polished from where my father squeezed past them on his way from the kitchen to the living room. The big wooden desk in my father's study was practically unusable, so laden it was with crystal paperweights, coin collections, old photographs, and medals from the war. But worst of all was my grandfather's collection of rabbit figurines. My father stashed the rabbits all around the house. They clustered on end tables and perched along the kitchen counters. They looked down imperiously from the tops of bookshelves and wedged themselves in among the books. They fell out in groups of two or three from infrequently opened cabinets and sat vigil on each step of the narrow staircase leading to the second floor. Everywhere you looked, there were rabbits. Everywhere you went, rabbit eyes stayed on you.

December came and with it, winter break. I would be heading home. "What day's your flight?" my father asked over the phone.

"Wednesday," I said.

"Come by the house when you can." Due to the state of my father's house, I always stayed at my mother's. "Maybe Friday."

Dallas cold was nothing compared to the East Coast, but it was still colder than I remembered. I had forgotten how crazy people in the neighborhood could get with the Christmas lights. On the way to my father's place, I passed a house with dozens of medium-sized Santa figurines, lit up from the inside and hanging from the trees. The little bearded men in their red suits didn't look cheerful to me. They looked helpless and forlorn, cloned against their will, all reduced to mere flimsy copies of whatever they might once have been.

At my father's house, the front door was open. Three of the antique vases were sitting out on the porch. I went inside. "Dad?"

My father appeared in the doorway of his study. His hair was sticking up on one side and he looked like he hadn't shaved in days. He was wearing an old blue T-shirt that now, many years since its initial purchase, fit tightly across his rounding belly. "Janie," he said. "Here. Take this." He handed me a long glass display case filled with old pennies.

"Why are the vases outside?"

"I was just making some room." He turned to a stray end table and picked up the wooden box that contained my grandfather's war medals. He stacked the box on top of the penny collection in my arms.

"Dad, what the hell? What are you doing with these?"

"I'm sorting things out, Janie. I'm figuring out what I need to give you."

"Give me? Why?"

He left the study and I followed him to the kitchen. He started opening and closing drawers. He scooted around a box of antique Christmas ornaments and made his way to the dining table. "Here." He picked up a pair of porcelain salt and pepper shakers shaped like rabbits. There were no markings on the shakers to distinguish which was salt and which was pepper; we simply had to guess between the two and take our chances. He set the rabbit shakers on top of my stack, where they rolled from side to side on their polished porcelain backs.

"Are you OK? Did something happen?"

"They're your grandfather's things, Janie. I want you to have them."

I looked down at the strange bounty in my arms. "You want me to have the penny collection, the war medals, and the salt shakers?"

"They're keepsakes," my father said as he picked his way back to his study. "You'll appreciate them someday."

I stood in the kitchen and studied the rabbits. They looked back at me, their painted eyes gleaming in the overhead light. My father wouldn't explain what he was doing. "That's all, that's all," he said. "I've got to get back to work here."

Back at my mother's house I dumped the items on the table in the foyer. I leaned over and gripped the table hard. My face felt hot; a lump formed in my throat. I imagined I might shake the table violently, knock all the precious heirlooms down onto the floor. I thought of those eggs from my dreams smashing to the ground and then reconstituting. I stood back up and picked up the rabbit salt shakers. Twin rabbits, perfect symmetry. According to the laws of physics, every object was interchangeable with its reflection. I held the rabbits up against the large decorative mirror hanging over the table. Nothing material would change, I thought, if I traded places with the version of me in the mirror. The only difference would be that things in the mirror would move backwards instead of forwards; things would repair themselves instead of always breaking. Lehman Brothers would be reconstituted; any pennies they had dropped would fly back up the length of the skyscraper; the poor maimed pedestrians' heads would be stitched back over their wounds and made whole. I would be left-handed instead of right, my left pinky calloused and gray from the pencil. I would be returning to my father's house right now, giving the rabbits back to him, and he would be returning the rabbits to my grandfather as my grandfather came back to life and my parents grew remarried. With the arrow of time thus reversed, my father would start acting less crazy and more normal as time went on. His mustache would grow back; we would be in Costco again; the wrench I had dropped would return to my hand. Physics would not care: From the perspective of supersymmetry, both worlds were perfectly equal. It was only from my meager human perspective that the differences between the mirrored world and my own felt so extreme.

I stared at my reflection. I put my hand up on the glass. Behind me, in the mirror, my mother stood watching me.

"Jane?" she said. "Sweetheart, what's wrong?"

I showed her the things my father had given me. "He's acting crazy! He's been acting crazy for months! He tells me about newspaper articles that don't make any sense and he expects me to understand. He gives me all this meaningless junk and he won't even say why. Why does he have to be like this? Why won't he ever explain what's going on?"

My mother picked up the rabbits on top of my stack. Little flecks of salt and pepper spilled out onto the table. Slowly, one by one, she examined the rabbits, the medals, the display case with the pennies. I hovered beside her with my hands fluttering at my side, worried she might drop something.

"There's something I should show you," my mother said at last.

She led me to the kitchen, where she fumbled through the drawers where she stuffed her stationery, her grocery lists, her yellowing calendars from many years past. I sat down at the table and she brought a stack of papers over to me.

"What is this?" I asked.

My mother sat down across from me. "You know how hard it is to get a straight answer out of your father."

I flipped through the papers. They were tax documents, accounting spreadsheets, business filings for the states of Texas, Delaware, and California. There was the tool company, the handbag company, the company that imported leather goods from Italy. On the backs of the pages my mother had scrawled notes in her loopy, lopsided script: citations and equivocations, equations and dollar signs, annotations punctuated with check marks. My father may have resisted her questions, but my mother sucked up information like a vacuum. Year after year, she ferreted away her findings, reviewing every page with her hawk's eye, mining every line item for its precious jewel of information and slowly, under intense interrogation, grinding it to dust under her ballpoint pen. This was my maternal inheritance, I thought: my mother's best attempt at a comprehensive view of my father's universe. Still, I couldn't make any sense of her notes. It seemed to me that she had analyzed and reanalyzed the papers so relentlessly that all reasoning bent back onto itself, such that everything came to mean its opposite.

"I don't understand," I said at last.

"The businesses have been failing for years, Jane. The tool company was the only one left."

"And now?"

"Now I guess that's gone, too."

I looked down at the papers. "Why didn't you ever say anything?"

"There's something else," my mother said. She moved her hands as she spoke, thin fingers curling in and out like crab legs. I kept imagining there was some slip of paper she was whipping back and forth before my eyes, lulling me relentlessly into agreement and submission. He'd mentioned a bank loan on the phone, she said. Payment due on January 1, she said. The little house mortgaged, the most precious heirlooms put up as collateral. He hadn't asked her for money—well, at least not directly. She supposed he was hoping she would offer him a loan on her own.

My throat felt raw. "I'm going to call him."

My mother placed her hand on mine. "I think it's best if you don't mention anything."

Across the table my phone caught the light from the lamp and beamed it up to the ceiling. "So what am I supposed to do? Just act like nothing has happened?"

"Jane," she said. "I'm sure he'll explain everything to you eventually."

A full week passed before my father told me he was moving from his house to a rented place across town. When I asked him why, he shrugged. "That house was always too big for me. I don't need all that space." I didn't ask him what he would do with the antique vases, the fine china, the rabbits. I assumed the bank would take it all. It would all end up in other houses, with other families, passed up the chain of fortune with no memory of its origin.

My mother screened my father's calls and rarely called him back. I detected in her an air of satisfaction whenever she flipped her phone to silent. *See,* she seemed to be saying, *your father was the bad parent all along.* If he was the failure, that made her the success. In my mother's head everything always summed to zero. For her, every win had to correspond to a loss, bad luck matching up to good as certainly as negative and positive charges. I had dreams of my father running through his little house, where the doorways around him transformed into portals that would suck him into other dimensions. "Take this, Janie, take this!" he'd say, tossing me pennies and medals and porcelain rabbits. What could I do? He wouldn't tell me anything. When I asked my mother if she thought he would be OK, she simply shrugged. "He's an adult," she said. "He's responsible for his own choices."

When the time came to return to school, I looked at the stack of my grandfather's heirlooms still sitting underneath the mirror in the foyer. As I picked through the items, I avoided meeting my reflection's gaze. To see myself there would remind me too much of that night when my mother had shown me the papers. I had wanted so desperately to understand what was happening with my father, but now that I knew, I wished I didn't. At last, I picked up the rabbit salt and pepper shakers and left the pennies and the war medals behind.

On the plane back east I took out my notebook and wrote down a list of questions I could not ask my father:

1. *What happened?*
2. *Will you be all right?*
3. *Is there something I can do?*

I stared at all my Greek symbols on the other side of the page. *Is there something I can do? Isn't there something I can do?* My graduate research stipend was considered among the most lucrative in the country, courtesy of a prestigious fellowship I had won the previous spring: $30,000 a year, doled out in quarters. I knew what was in my savings account: $2,400. I ran the math in my head. $2,400 would not cover even a single mortgage payment. And $30,000 a year would never be enough to solve my father's problems.

When I arrived at my apartment, I spent the evening dreaming up strategies. A better job, more money, taking up online poker. Selling my old clothes, tutoring high school physics, finding the people on Craigslist who would offer money in exchange for sex. How did other people make money, anyway? How was it that anyone ever came to be rich? *I could strike oil,* I thought. *My grandfather did.* But how could I even know where to start digging?

The next morning I returned to the dead professor's office. There was my name on the door. My father's name, my grandfather's name: *Fields, Fields, Fields.* I wanted to tear the sign down, rip it into little pieces and shove them down into the trash where no one would ever see my name again. Instead I went inside and shut the door behind me. I sat down on the floor and put my arms around my knees.

My path through graduate school had seemed so reasonable back in September. I had planned for my most likely future. I had imagined that life was like a bell curve: that good and bad luck lay only at the ends, with vanishingly small likelihood, and most everyone spent whole lifetimes in the middle, where things were normal. I had thought that my life would unfold like a fairy tale—that as the arrow of time moved forward, so would my own fortunes always move up. Now I had no sense of how the past and the future might unfurl on either side of me. Now the bell curve seemed flattened, with bad luck raining down on everyone no matter where they stood. Disaster was a possibility for everyone in the world: for Lehman Brothers in their skyscraper, for me in my little office, for my father in his house stuffed with a dead man's things. There was no bell curve, no happy middle zone. There was only win or lose, and no guarantee of survival.

The young professor and I are children, I had thought that morning when I found the first newspaper. For all our mathematical proficiency, we could not define the complex derivative. We could not explain what effect the price of copper might have on a human life. We didn't even know how to pronounce Lehman Brothers. How could we have failed to recognize what the *Lee-muns* of the world so clearly understood? *We thought money was incidental, but it is fundamental,* I thought. An insight as profound as the shift from classical mechanics to the quantum reality: Occasionally, it really does turn out that everything you thought you knew about the world is wrong. So here it was at last, reality intruding on the theory wing: Janie Fields, still five years old at twenty-three, learning, for the first time, that there is no intelligence so vast that it can shield a girl from market forces. The market cares nothing for brilliance, or even individuality. From the height of Wall Street's offices, each person on the ground is interchangeable with any other, all equally likely to be struck on the head and killed by a penny cast carelessly off the roof.

Newton, they say, also had to have the truth conked into him by an apple in descent.

I wished I hadn't left my grandfather's pennies at home. I would need them now. There was some chance, maybe, that I could sell them on eBay—or spend them, at least, if it came to that. But of course those pennies would never be enough. I needed some way to make money, real money, enough money to make sure no *Fields* would ever again find themselves so vulnerable to collapse. *If I had money, then everything could go back to the way it was,* I thought. My father could go back to his little house. He could recover my grandfather's cherished possessions. He could buy all his companies back, just like before. *If I had enough money,* I thought, *I could reverse the arrow of time.*

I looked up at the dead professor's papers stacked all around the desk and stood from the floor. My head rushed. The blood pounded in my ears. A disaster had happened—why not a miracle? Half of our department's graduates wound up working on Wall Street, after all. Finance always had need for physics' battle-hardened theories. Maybe the dead professor had come to some solution, some perfect equation that would allow me to vacuum money out of the stock market like my mother had vacuumed up information. Maybe the answers I needed were right here in this dead man's office. I had to believe it—I had, at the very least, to try. Something in all these old papers might yet save me.

I sat down in the dead professor's chair. I pulled the papers to me and began to read. I made notes in the margins. I reproduced his calculations in the notebook at my side. My right hand went gray with pencil smears as I slipped into the kind of trance I knew well from my supersymmetry calculations. I was burning up with the desire to know, to understand. As my eyes ran over the pages, I started thinking in a different kind of language. My lines of thought expanded forwards and backwards, turning the equations over and over on themselves so I could come to know them from the inside out. From three dimensions I expanded out to four, to five, out to infinity. Mathematics, in my hands, enlarged the world beyond all human comprehension. I felt huge, expanded, and so the word came to me: *Fields.* Broad like a field, open like a field, rich like a field where seeds could grow. I felt the truth germinate in me, take shape on the page. I could almost see it, halfway feel it: Through these equations, the dead professor resurrected in my hands.

I stayed looking through the papers until morning. I woke up to find the sun in my eyes and the young professor tapping at the door. The dead professor's papers had left smudges on my cheek where I slept. I sat up and blinked over my notes. As I scanned the pages, I realized they made no sense. My passing faith had come to nothing: The dead professor's papers were just equations upon equations, nonsense math that led nowhere. He had not come back to life in order to explain the world to me—he was as dead as ever and had nothing to explain. And I? I had focused all my powers, all my native brilliance, all my mathematical training, and still I had failed. My spells were impotent, my charms empty, the enchantment over, once and for all. I wiped the pencil smudges from my cheek. *Let it be over, then,* I thought. I had tried the physics. Now I would try something else.

I told the young professor I would have the new calculations ready for him by the afternoon. I went to the library and checked out several volumes on quantitative finance. When I returned to the office, I set my new books on the dead professor's desk and swept all of his papers into the trash.

Of course, quantitative practice is not really where the business of finance gets done. Money on Wall Street is made not in finely wrought predictions but in backroom deals, in shrewdly spotted loopholes, in cheating. But if the financiers desired mathematics' crystal sheen— the high gloss of alleged genius, the pure white porcelain glare—then I would give it to them. I would do what I did best. I would learn the math. *It's never the math—bad or otherwise,* my father had said. But he had not seen the situation as I did. My equations could not hold the full weight of the world's truth, but they could yet dazzle. They could blind an audience of outsiders unsure of how things really worked. They could paper over the truth, turn good to bad and bad to good— and I, of all people, knew the power of manipulated symmetry.

The bank foreclosed on my father's house. I heard the news from my mother. I kept talking to my father on the phone, talking about everything except the truth of what was actually going on. I continued my work in the theory wing, waiting out the years for the financial industry to recover. I spent my small research stipend carefully. I took vitamin D tablets and ate rice and beans. I patched my jeans. I drove the speed limit. I stayed away from black ice.

I studied the markets constantly. I memorized the derivation of the Black-Scholes equation. I learned that every financial instrument has its opposite: the call and the put, the straddle and the strangle, the butterfly and the condor—perfect symmetries unfolding like principles of physical law. I put my knowledge to the test and started trading options. In my first week I made two hundred dollars.

At every step I imagined my success was just luck; I stayed vigilant to the possibility of a reversal in the trend. I knew I would never feel financially secure so long as I was playing my bush-league game, carefully placing bets with only the money I could afford to lose. True security would require that I trade a lot more money, preferably someone else's. I kept my eyes open to opportunities. When the hedge fund recruiters finally came back to campus, I knew more about the theoretical mechanics of the stock market than anyone in my graduate program. One hedge fund booked me a flight to New York for an interview, and I spent the last of my trading profits on an expensive new suit. When I packed my bag, I took one of the rabbit salt shakers with me, for luck.

I had the rabbit in the pocket of my suit jacket when I arrived at the hedge fund's offices. The elevator on the way up was walled entirely in mirrors. Inside, I gripped hold of the rabbit and met my reflection's gaze. *Two of us came into this elevator,* I thought. *But only one of us will leave.* I would step through the elevator's doors, into the high office, to join the men who spoke their twisted language of securities, commodities, and futures. My reflection would stay behind, trapped behind the elevator's glossy mirror, moving backwards through time while I went forwards, our dual reality cleaved, at last, in half.

Strange: when I got back to my hotel in the city, the rabbit wasn't in my pocket anymore. I pulled my new suit jacket apart looking for it. It wasn't in any of the pockets, not the outside pockets or the inside pockets or the little false pocket at the lapel. It must have fallen out somewhere, I thought. It must now be somewhere on the street of New York City, kicked from block to block, street to gutter, its little ears cracked and its polished body gritty, the salt from its belly spilling out into the road.

My father lives in an apartment now—much smaller than the little house the bank took from him. I tell him: "Dad, let me help you get something bigger, something closer to town." But he says the apartment suits him fine. He no longer has the vases, the silver platters, the china teacups—though just the other day I opened a cabinet in his kitchen and found four of the old rabbits staring back at me. He's still working all the time—his desk is full of papers—but the details of his projects, he never discloses. One night a few years ago, I googled the name of his tool company to see what might have become of it. My eyes glazed over before I could finish reading the bankruptcy filing.

In the summers my dad and I watch baseball games on TV. It's a pastime we've shared since I was very young, ever since he explained to me the whole concept of moneyball. "All right, Janie," he'll say, "what's today's over-under?" We make bets sometimes—not with real money, just with little odds and ends from around the house, washer plates and loose screws—our version of poker chips. Yesterday, we were watching the game on his old rabbit ears TV when he went to get something from the kitchen.

"You need anything?" he asked.

"I'm all right," I said. On TV the camera panned the crowd. It zoomed in on a couple kissing. It zoomed in on a row of men wearing identical bright blue hats. There were five of them; the hats spelled out something I couldn't quite decipher. I drew closer to the screen to read the letters, and there, behind the men, I saw a man who looked just like my father. He was leaning down to talk to the child beside him, who was hidden behind the men in the blue hats. He leaned down towards the child conspiratorially, pointing out at the broad green field, explaining the rules of the game. I pressed my hand up to the glass. "Dad?"

My dad appeared in the doorway. "I'm here, Janie. I'm right here."

Amy Fleury

Wishful Thinking

If only the stars had aligned better at your birth
or you arrived on a day luckier than a Wednesday.
What if you could be sure that love's stronger than death?

How different it all would be if only you'd left
ten minutes later. Why on earth didn't you wait?
If only that Mercury had not crossed your path

or you'd met a red light. Oh, to have been so blessed!
You wondered how far into the lake you could wade.
What if no one had saved you when you passed your depth?

For days you watched the hurricane churning the Gulf,
weighing whether to stay or leave or leave or stay.
If only the storm veered to the west, what a gift

that would've been, but not for Texas—just a half-
turn and the debris could have flown another way.
What if it was stranger rather than neighbor who wept

before a roofless house? And your baby whose breath
never came easy no matter how hard you'd pray.
If only you could swap this for that other life,
as if what you know of love would save you from grief.

Sara Henning

Ghost Story

Savannah, my mother would say,
*so beautiful General Sherman could not watch
it burn.* Perhaps this is why we stayed

in this city of rain-torched oaks
two years after my father died, Spanish moss
draping the branches like pashmina over

a dead girl's shoulders. Yamacraws
called it *itla-okla,* threaded it into ropes
or blankets to warm the haunches

of horses. *Barbe Espagnol*: French
colonists mocking the beards of Spanish
conquistadors. But when she said it,

my mother, I believed it—*Savannah,
so beautiful, so beautiful*—like that afternoon,
1984, on the baseball diamond,

when I, four years old, clung to Laurie,
acid-washed jean shorts gripping her
freckled thighs. She was Beth's daughter,

thirteen, piercing her ears with ice
and safety pins, and she watched me when
our mothers left us to sip Dos Equis

and suck the flesh from lime rinds,
to harp about men or the latest of Laurie's
disasters—Laurie, scaling

the downspout from the bathroom
window to meet boys in the backs of cars.
Laurie slinking upstairs at twilight,

her underwear in her purse. Her red hair,
I remember its helix curled against my face
when I wrapped my arms around her.

Some days I traced the dark circles
under her eyes. Laurie, she clings to me
now like Spanish moss, that wet,

heavy hunger. Two days after she went
missing, they found her raped, throat slit,
heart-shaped holes cut into the breasts

of her Pink Floyd T-shirt. A car's
slashed leather, the heat-ripped metal
of a trash can off Tremont

which held her—no one told me
how she left the world. My mother
only said Laurie had *gone away,*

was *never coming back.* Cops
don't find killers, I'd learn too soon,
in cases like this, for girls who scuff

the toes of their sneakers
when they dance or ash a smoke,
Saturday blooming before them like

a heaven that could seize them up—
raped girl, ghost story. Even Sherman
would not burn it down.

Sara Henning

A Brief History of Skin

in the infinite meadows of heaven,
Blossomed the lovely stars, the forget-me-nots of the angels.

—Henry Wadsworth Longfellow, "*Evangeline: A Tale of Acadie*"

Return it, the moles constellating my right shoulder,
deep brown poultice. My husband once kissed
his way into its world. Bless it, biopsy knife

swiping through my flesh, my faith. Unname it
Nevus Spilus, little Andromeda galaxy stretching my skin,
its infinite halo of dark matter. Unwhisper the word

melanoma, those sleepless weeks I swore
it glimmered, debris from an exploded star.
Unclench my hand from its jigger of vodka,

uncurl my husband's grip from my shoulder.
Unwhisper the word *cancer, mother.*
Unburden my skin from the blazing Utah May,

where, one spring, the sun ravaged me.
Untangle me from recklessness, untruss
the tumors from my mother's blood.

Return her record player's needle shirring
through scarred vinyl, Mick Jagger throating
blues through her house on Victory Drive.

Rebridle her hair to its messy knot,
unveil the dime-sized mole on the back of her neck.
Give them back, my father's words for it—

forget-me-not of the angels, plush field of stars.
Give her back her body when she still loved
my father, when I still moved within her.

But if you can give me nothing, God,
return her name for me—little one,
infinite meadow of heaven.

Megan Borocki

Field Notes No. 3

It all started with a tibia blocking the beds of beans.
Over time, a slow regaining of limbs: an arm,
seven ribs from the left side, a foot, and in her
mouth they found the molt of a cicada,
two underground nymphs who joined forces.
The farmer didn't know how she got there,
how long she had been swimming in his soil,
no whispers of a missing woman towns over. Just
silence that comes at the end of a sentence.
The town was quick to forget. It's easy to move on
to the next drowned girl, the next dead thing.
The soybeans in that plot grew twice as green
so the farmer's kids got clean shoelaces for church
and bellies full of bone-sweet Necco wafers.
The children planted pink ones in the soil
where she was found, little rituals birthing
up each year the beans came back. Quiet,
the stuck pieces of her: a left foot, shoulder
blades, hip plates tangled in roots each season
till a family of souls grew, snugged close
among the warming dirt, and if the children
listened closely, smashed ear to dirt, they heard,
maybe, a wind chime sounding deep.

Robert P. Kaye

Spaceship in a Bottle

Dear Tanner,

The *Millennium Falcon* in a bottle broke while I was cleaning your "design workshop." I thought you should know as soon as you returned from Jordan's, since we agreed to be transparent about sticky issues from now on. I know you'll be pissed, but it has been three years and you've only managed to fit part of the model inside the bottle, while a layer of dust has accumulated like a space Pompeii. You know how I hate messes.

I prioritized cleaning the design workshop last, even though it occupies our kitchen table where I used to do jigsaw puzzles after a hard day working customer service. Which is still super stressful BTW, even for someone with my "accommodating temperament." As your Primary Life and Business Partner, I acknowledge agreeing to stay at my "menial job" to facilitate cash flow while you made us "stupid rich" with Spaceship in a Bottle, Inc. Not that I had a choice, since you'd already told your boss you'd rather belly flop into a vat of battery acid than install another windshield. Meanwhile, the business hasn't exactly "jumped to warp drive" as promised. Yes, I acknowledge not getting that in writing.

Cleaning the kitchen got me thinking about high school, when you were a quarterback and I was an aspiring cheerleader. When I caught your passes in the park, you said "you complete me" and tackled me so we could roll around in the grass. And he scores! And the crowd goes C-R-A-Z-Y! Never mind that you only played eighteen minutes in your senior year and I never made the cheer squad, like Jordan did. We were in pursuit of cosmic possibilities, together.

While vacuuming around the bookshelves, I discovered a clump of bent cardboard from that time you shook up two of my jigsaw puzzles in the same box to prove that the pieces were all the same, just with different pictures. You were trying to make a point about interchangeable parts. When it turned into a mashed Frankenpicture, you threw it all at the bookshelves and went to Jordan's to "resolve shopping cart issues" on the website. I tried salvaging the pieces, since puzzles were out of the budget with our credit cards maxed on models, X-Acto knives, glassblowing equipment, and, of course, web design. Today I threw the puzzles in the dumpster, realizing they would never be whole again.

Vacuuming around my exercise bike/clothes rack made me remember my list of pending items that you often recap, including my business degree, cosplay costumes, losing weight, getting a promotion, buying a house, and starting a family. I don't need to hear again how I should adopt Jordan as a role model for entrepreneurial success. I did that for you after cleaning the mirror.

Scrubbing the stains on the couch reminded me of discovering you "inadvertantly'" fucking my "bestie" Jordan there. I still don't see how her "taking care of your needs" because I'm too stressed out for sex is a "benefit to me." Especially when I know that Spaceship in a Bottle is her only web design client, which means I'm supporting both of you.

Stripping the bedsheets for laundry, I realized the answer to your proposal to "combine the best of both worlds and take our relationship to the next level!" by including Jordan is a hard no. I don't believe that our parts are interchangeable. Forcing them together will result in bent pieces that end up in the dumpster (which is where the sheets are, BTW). Call me "morally hidebound" all you want.

Cleaning the kitchen table/design studio, it occurred to me that if I commanded a spaceship imprisoned inside a glass bubble, my mission would be to break free. I wrapped the *Millennium Falcon* prototype in one of your Comicon T-shirts and smashed it between two bookshelf cinder blocks. I repeated the experiment with the *Battlestar Galactica, Serenity, Red Dwarf,* and various generations of starship *Enterprise.* You know how I hate incompletion. The smashing is a real selling point. Call it market research. You're welcome.

Unfortunately, I didn't have time to finish cleaning. Maybe Jordan will step up in exchange for my equity interest, which I hereby relinquish. I am moving to my sister's place in a galaxy far, far away, embracing the customer service truth that you can't make everybody happy.

You don't complete me anymore, which is infinitely sad. But then completion is more my thing than yours.

Your ex-Primary Life and Business Partner,

Rachel

Ric Hoeben

Alice

On the third hour of painting the porch ceiling in the robin's-egg blue strokes, the girls stopped for their first cigarette. It was Maggie and Miriam. Miriam, the daughter, was sixteen and little accustomed to smoking tobacco with her mother. She had made the great promise to Maggie to help with the painting chore for the day, and in doing so, would be rewarded with a heap of Beaufort stew for dinner and a trip to the mainland in the morning to finally see the old Flagg girl's grave.

It had been during a balmy weekday morning when Miriam sat in the day school, sketching out seahorses on her beloved notepad, when she first began to hear anything of the Flagg girl. They were, she realized, of the same critical age of sixteen, and to think Miss Flagg had been trying to get married in her life–Miriam had never even had a boy look at her in that way, and she felt that cooking and sleeping with a male was something a far off for her, but Miss Flagg had lived in a much different time era, as Miriam's History Lecturer informed the school class. Flagg had wanted this poor boy from way over in Johnsonville, a tanned, rough boy, a boy who was bruised and who smirked his way through existence.

The historical Flaggs were gentry and did not cotton to their daughter marrying herself off to the Johnsonville boy, the peasant laborer. The Flagg girl, it seemed, had received a promise ring from the boy, and the girl's older brother had every intention of finding the jewelry piece given for marriage and taking it, crushing it, obliterating it, or throwing it in the marshes to wash away and never come back to do bother to the family.

Miriam left school at the closing bell on the day she had learned the great history story, had gotten herself a box of taffy and worked her way down to the bluestems and seagulls and waited for her friend, the old Geechee woman, who came combing the beach in the mid-afternoons with her shoat, a shoat she was immensely proud of, and understandably so, because the darling pig could talk and guess and speculate and suggest and divinate to those not too proud to sit down in the coarse sand and give ear.

There she sat, young Miriam, with the shoat, feeding him an orange taffy, then a strawberry one, then a nice green one, as the Geechee woman looked for wonderful shells in the surf, no one around nearby but a man trying for flounder some paces off in the distance

The hog gave over to great talking:

"You must find the girl's ring," he started.

"And you mean Miss Flagg's?" Miriam asked. "But I would not know where to start."

He snorted. "It is a tiny item to even try after, for sure, sitting somewhere off in the Atlantic Ocean, but go ahead and pray to Jesus the Christ and to your fairy, and sooner—"

"But this is just impossible," Miriam stammered. "Are you sure it was not crushed and buried? Are you sure it is even freaking out here in the surf?"

The pig smiled a warm look. "Yes," he said, "I have heard of it—but more importantly, I have seen it, just below where the jellyfish pass by and the crabs scurry. I promise you as hard as I can promise a listener, Miriam."

Miriam breathed deeply.

The swine said even more: "Go and take the old ring to her grave at the church. You will find her tomb, where many have sat and talked to the girl's soul for comfort. Where many have left her some beads, and crosses, all the shiny trinkets and lovely morsels."

And it was so that Miriam made it a personal mission for herself. She told Maggie her mother, she told the church rector. She told God himself. That marriage ring simply had to be found.

Presently Miriam peeled another jumbo shrimp and licked the Old Bay from it. Maggie, her mother, was having Rioja wine and enjoying a small piece of yellow corn.

"When we get to the grave, Mama," Miriam broached, "will you help me kneel and pray to Flaggy, to her?"

The girl's mother grinned. "Of course I will. We can talk to our fairies, and to Jesus the Christ. Surely something nice will come of it."

She stopped for a sip of the red wine. "Miriam, I am so proud of you for wanting to get her old ring back to her. You know, many people have tried. It has become something of a beautiful tradition. Flaggy died when she was your age, soul-sick and missing her man, that poor dude kept away from her like that, I declare."

As Miriam began clearing the dishes, Maggie lit up a long menthol. Leonard Bernstein was on the stereo, and outside the wind blew through the palms. Miriam felt a discovery tingle in her teeth, something different and new and not unlikable; she felt, then, like she was someone's summer girl, and she could see the angels coming down, like the waves crashing on the ground.

Michaella Thornton

Why a Mother Teaches Her Daughter to Shovel Snow

1.

Where I grew up near Kansas City, Missouri, I shoveled snow and mowed lawns and changed my truck's brake pads with my father. I did these things not to prove that girls were capable, but because that's what you do in the lower Midwest when your former-jock father, a power-and-light dispatcher who listened to too much Rush Limbaugh, wished he'd had a son first instead of a smart-mouthed daughter.

I know where my three-year-old daughter gets her stubborn optimism, her need to be out in this single-digit St. Louis cold with her mother, who is, this particular winter, almost always shoveling snow. I respect my child's resolve and kindness and sense of joyous solidarity because snow can be fun and is not just a Sisyphean exercise in moving shovelfuls of frozen water from one surface to the next. In fact, my daughter often reminds me to put down the shovel, to lie in the snow with her, to create these ephemeral, translucent wings together.

But beyond keeping her warm, I want my daughter to have a childhood, something I didn't really have as the eldest daughter of four. Instead, I was one who took care of my siblings every other weekend when our father lashed out at us in anger.

Anger at a light left on in the upstairs bedroom or a tub of margarine placed on the wrong refrigerator shelf. Anger when I read books indoors instead of playing softball outside or offered up facts when he raged on in his opinions. Anger because my mother left him first, and then our stepmother second. Anger that no one seemed to appreciate how hard he worked, even though we all knew what overtime and time-and-a-half were and what everything cost before we knew how to drive, how to walk away, how to leave him like our mothers.

My girlhood, my identity even, was forged in trying to be "good," to not displease, to read a room and its inhabitants' intentions and emotions before anyone ever opened their mouths, to walk on eggshells already crushed by my father's anger.

When it snowed, I shoveled and salted steps without being asked. I cleared surfaces for a man who blamed everyone else for the destruction left in his path.

2.

On this freezing February evening, I wait for my young daughter to fall asleep before I clear the driveway to ready our daily journey to preschool and then work.

Truth be told, I am exhausted and fall asleep with her snuggled in my arms. When I wake, it's almost eleven p.m. The temperature outside clocks zero degrees Fahrenheit I put on a thermal zip-up over my sweater and leggings and pull on long wool socks, a hooded winter coat, warm gloves my ex left behind, my Marge Gunderson hat, and my beloved pair of insulated and waterproof Kamik Men's Fargo boots.

3.

When a marriage ends, some women buy cordless drills, weighted blankets, vibrators, wine, gym memberships, self-help books, dating app subscriptions, jewelry, or a grand vacation. For me, the fall after my ex leaves, the first thing I buy are big-ass snow boots.

Feeling stuck is one of my greatest fears, greater than being neglected, greater than being abused, far greater than being abandoned and left to fend for myself. I've survived this much and more, and, at the end of the day, the wish I want most is to know I can take good care of myself and my daughter.

So, I wish for boots which can withstand temperatures down to minus forty degrees. Boots that make me feel comfortable on slick surfaces, like I was built for shoveling snow uphill in unforgiving weather. Like I was a woman made of salt and steel and not some lonesome girl forged in solitude and ice.

When I wear these boots, I know I'll be OK. My daughter will be OK. We'll both be OK; more than OK, actually. She will see her tough-ass mother outside the dining room window shoveling snow. Her inheritance, I pray, is she will know how to dig herself out of a challenging situation. She will never doubt that she is loved, she is brave—she is free.

4.

At night there is a faint glow of gold emanating from my neighbors' porch lights. Two-bedroom, one-bath brick bungalows from the late 1920s and newly built half-a-million-dollar homes sit side by side in this suburban St. Louis neighborhood, separated only by middle-class chain-link fences or high-dollar privacy barriers.

The world is quiet. No one else makes the muffled scraping sound of metal on pavement late at night like I do.

I leave the back door open with the glass patio door shut on the off chance my three-year-old daughter wakes to use the restroom or tries to find me, which she often does when I leave her bed to wash dishes, fold laundry, read, binge watch a series, or try in vain to sleep in my own bed until she crawls in beside me, arms outstretched.

She has grown used to the boundary of my body, nestling her warmth into mine, and I will not lie: Falling asleep next to her is my greatest comfort, even with her feet jabbing me in the stomach or her face mere inches from mine come morning when she announces, "It's wake-up time!"

But this time when I sneak away from her, I do so to clear the snow off of the back porch and to make a salted trail to my compact car, which is idling in the driveway with half a foot of snow on top. I want to make sure the engine will start come morning, that the ice and snow don't become so heavy in their accumulation that clearing our way in the morning will be harder than it has to be. So, I retrieve a broom to sweep off the car's hood, to do what I can now.

And as I approach the glass door, I see my daughter's reflection—golden hair loose and wavy, rainbow-striped pajamas, bare feet, eyes scrunched up in tears. I open the door and hug her and tell her I'll be right back, to stay put, and then run to turn off the car's engine.

"Oh, honey," I say upon return, scooping her up in the cold mudroom, "please go back to bed."

"I had a bad dream," she says, crying, as I carry her back to her bedroom. "I need you. Where were you?"

"I was shoveling snow," I whisper, pulling the covers up and over her small body, kissing her forehead, her baby cheeks. "I am right here. I would never leave you."

"But I wanted to shovel with you," she says, tears warming my face.

I hold her until she falls back to sleep, and I breathe in her scent—sweet orange and vanilla shampoo, dryer sheets, applesauce, innocence.

Tomorrow we will shovel snow together, not out of obligation or fear or a desire to create order out of a mess my child did not create. No, I will give her a different birthright: a pale blue shovel and sturdy hot-pink snow boots and an innate belief in her strength and worth. That perhaps, just maybe, I will help her uncover a path I did not get to take myself. That if I am lucky and work hard enough, I will be a mother who unburies her grief so her child might walk surely, swiftly, unencumbered.

Vladislav Hristov

διάβολος —the greek word for devil

carries the meaning
"the one who slanders"
i observe the neighborhood kids
how they split into teams
the strongest mandates
which team the weak ones should join
then the slander
among the players begins
war exists
on the same principle

☾

the soldier loading the cannon
wears thick canvas gloves
during the entire war
his hands stay clean
everyone dreams
to have it that way
falling sleep with clean hands
and waking up the same way

☾

most of all
the bomb shelter resembles a womb
jonah left the whale long ago
they switched places
without us noticing
now the whale is inside jonah
and every second
opens its mouth

Vladislav Hristov

☾

the wires are meant for swallows
the sparrows prefer
landing on a fence
the owls love chimneys
the storks—electric poles
the wounded airplane
can't be a chooser
of a landing place

Translated from the Bulgarian by Katerina Stoykova

Marin Bodakov

Final Draft

now we're dressing the corpse
and having difficulties with the buttons

now we're priming the corpse
and sniffing shadows in the air

now we're carrying out the corpse
and covering it with dirt and branches

we sense the lack of organs
with which to mourn

now

Translated from the Bulgarian by Katerina Stoykova

Meg Tuite

She Got the Her on Him Who They Still Speak of in Relapsed Gender

News gunned across every church from Springfield to Mississippi after the birth of Abigail. Her mother Nancy's womb belted the length of the Union States. When her water broke, she drained more than three thousand square miles through central Illinois and flash flood corn and pumpkin seeds her father had planted. When Nancy farted, she could manage a perfect C and A-minor chord depending on the time of day. Some say the infant was longer than a train traveling through 180 cities and seven states. Others said the Sangamon River hissed and spectacled over 264 miles to the Illinois River. Size was the least of Nancy's worries. Shortly after the birth, objects started nose-diving out of her vagina: several empty bottles of brandy, most of someone's cattle, a dozen cats, a few pigs, a horse, a turkey, a goat, and more than a crate full of Bibles.

When Nancy's melancholy descended on Abby, the littlest of three children, Nancy was listless, trembling, and a stench bayed over her breath of cattle, sheep, and horses. The doctor said it was milk sickness after they tried to get her out of bed. When she vomited without stop and an odor of chemicals presumed off the skin, the doctor prepared the family for the worst.

Thomas, the imperious, fuddled father of this tribe, was a farmer, a carpenter, but couldn't read or write. He was forthright in his rage, humiliated any scribbled page that dared question him. He sequestered another wife, Sarah, who lived three cabins over, a few weeks after Nancy shriveled.

Abby grew up in the countryside eating five meals a day beneath legs surging upwards toward new horizons, over mountains, long faces, furies, evasions; she grew and grew, and once again, grew. Never cared that a suitor could find her, she bent over rooms to enter them. The younger brother died. The sister had notches in the wood of the door frame. Thomas, their father, threw his knife up into the wood beams. That's as near as Abby would ever come to a measurement.

Abby's second mother, Sarah, came with a pack of children. She took a liking to Abby, whose clothes were stitched for midgets and kept Abby from standing straight for years. Sarah put her needlework aside and started sewing clothes out of women's quilts and scraps from clucking pouches of Kentucky tongues. Sarah found the perfect log and set it along Abby's back and between her armpits. Abby rose into the sky, one of the first true phoenix of the 1800s.

And so why, the subterfuge of gender? Abby racked through the headwinds of jobs available for females? Domestic servant, farm worker, tailor, and washerwoman. Son of no gun, she said. I'm planting oak tree feet in the goddamned White House. I am to be a president.

Abagail Abe Lincoln became the sixteenth president and first woman president. News swam its way to the Carolinas where Andrea Andrew Johnson waited her turn. After that, it became hersay:

> Ulalia Ulysses Grant
> Ruth Rutherford Hayes
> Janey James Garfield

Leigh Camacho Rourks

Sixty-Five Days After the Nuns Began to Disappear, Alina Is Found; Her Daughter Is Not

It is not the thick tube the color of eggshells in coffee grounds feeding on her, feasting on her, that makes her finally snap up and listen to the man saying, *NO*, screaming in her face, "We have to leave. Now. Now. Now."

The pain of THEY at her torso, that sharp pulling below her belly button is not what slams her into motion. Not the way THEY bites, suckles. Not the way THEY tears, because she hasn't *just* woken up, hasn't *just* noticed the slick, hungry alien thing dragging behind her every step in the compound. She's been awake for days.

Weeks.

Letting THEY.

She opened herself to THEY's hunger, after all. Slipped silk pants down across hips, her arms heavy with the leader's prayers—doing this, all of this, while her mind, a camera, moved farther, farther, farther, up, out. Panoramic, wide shot, motion blur.

It's not the man's panting—"They're coming. They know," or "Damnit, Alina, see me. See. Me."—that pushes her pupils to pinpricks, tightens muscle in the seconds before explosive motion.

Alina?

Not his face that frees her (this man she maybe remembers loving) or the pearl of blood on his sparse eyelashes, the flood of red across his dark iris. The wounds. Not his hands, their panic. Not the way they bruise and bleed as he tries to pry the beating, feeding tube from her body. Not even the knife he snaps open. Not its silver flash.

> *It may be her
> name.*

Not the moment the tube burrows deeper, defiant, ravenous. Not the way pain floods her with adrenaline, endorphins. Not THEY's heartbeat, the sound of a sonogram or waterfall, her heartbeat.

These things are *not* her birth of fight/flight.

> *It may not.*

It's not the women down the hall, each tubed and robed, reciting the affirmations. The women she came here—here, here, here in THEY's lair—to free. Not the men in the next building, tubed, robed, reciting. Not the children, tubed, robed, reciting.

Not her daughter, tubed, robed.

> *Alina.*

Reciting.

> *The girl's name?
> Her girl?*

Not the words (the cadence of prayers) spilling from her lips, lies sounding like supple sanctuary.

> *Or maybe not.*

Words she hears. Does not hear. Words she says. Does not say. Over, over. Again, again. The prayer THEY taught her through the tube: "I will feed the peace. A piece of me. I will love the love. A love of me."

> *Someone's name?*

The way the words taste like paradise.

> *His name? This*
> *yelling, tugging,*
> *cutting   man?*
> *Alina?*

It is, instead, the hole in the ceiling, the blast hole. Air, air, air following the smoke, the spark.

Or more accurately, what hurls the camera that is her consciousness back into her brain, snapping it in place, howling her into being, what sparks a neuron and another, another, what sets a synapse on fire, spreads flames, what bursts her into *being* is every single thing that gap, that blast hole lets in.

> *No, not his name.*

The smell of clover, green, sweet. The warm stretch of wind, thick with humidity. The whip of her own hair across her lip. Hot light climbing bare, bruised, blackened feet.

> *Alina.*

And then, at once, she has jerked the knife from him. Not thinking. Jabbing. Jabbing into the soft of her meat, near the tube.

> *A body's name.*

Cut up, cut under. Cut UP. CUT UNDER. CUTCUTCUTCUT.

Cut the body, cut Alina free.

Stefan Manasia

The Salvation of the Species

We are the salvation of the species, Irina.
So did the scientists in my head tell me.
In the Southern hemisphere of the new planet, they claim,
Dr. Mortex is gathering his divisions,
preparing the death containers.
If in the atolls, from camps, he had kidnapped teenagers,
he is now sequestering adamantine virgins:
tribes spat on the equator, in the desert.
He is ripping off the testicles of the escaped urban dwellers
over the ray barrier (sick with endorphinitis,
fear, curiosity).

It is just us
under the city's dome
alone and fragrant,
of a hallucinatory tenderness.

We are on the train driven by Artemidorus the mechanic.
We are in the UFO flown by the orchids.
We are at the bottom of an ether well.
We are floating inside the sandworm.
We are naked and wearing bat fur on a beach
with a perfectly set temperature.
We are synchronously flinching during the induced sleep,
5,447 Earth years, on the board of the galactic Ore Tanker
(the pride of the fleet).

Stefan Manasia

☾

We are the salvation of the species, Irina, trust me.
The scientists in my brain, in their fireproof suits,
could barely tell me this,
in a final, frightening message.

Translated From the Romanian by Clara Burghelea

Michael Rogner

Los Farallones

We lived in a house full of mice
and a ghost who climbed the night stairs
to lean on your chest and inhale old names.
The mice we fed to gulls. The ghost
we learned from old journals arrived in 1972.
Always the same trip. Up the stairs. Lean on chest.
Three or four times a year and we never learned
if she fulfilled her mission. Perhaps
that's what we all want. Contact. Confirmation.
A wheezy gasp from the precious host.
On clear days San Francisco rose on the horizon
like the first glimpse of Rome
as the hordes backed you down
so we turned and faced west
where once a body floated by
devoid of agency. We tagged
sharks and counted seals and netted birds
to attach numbers to their feet.
At night the cosmos dripped. Stargazer
starlight space stuff streaking.
At night I listened to twenty-five thousand gull screams
breaking up and then coalescing like frogs. We were surrounded
by death. Dead birds. Dead seals turned into bright pink
slicks floundering without a hind quarter
with the patient shark below. The body
we named Bob wore a leather jacket and wingtips.
While two government agencies argued jurisdiction
Bob sailed over the Continental Shelf. Orcas

came and no sharks were seen for a year.
Pacific white-sided dolphins raced our little boat
wondering why we were capturing jellyfish
in old yogurt containers. We slit the ling cod bellies
to find tiny coffins lined within. We enumerated it all.
We had one radio station and zero internets. Every four
weeks a boat arrived with supplies and old newspapers
where we read about which wars we were starting
and the jumbled mess inhabiting the Giants bullpen.
During one World Series the wind blew from shore
and everywhere to the west winking sunlight crept our way.
Not sunlight but thousands of ballooning spiders
on their own evolutionary thread. Not spiders
sailing but little bodies doomed and fearless.

Mike White

People Food

Another evening, Death,
with you
whimpering to be fed
people food straight
from the table
like a coddled dog.

Given my bed
is your bed,
I'll sleep when you sleep,
and you'll run down rabbits
and I'll dream up God.

Reviews

Quarantine Highway by Millicent Borges Accardi. McAllen, Texas: FlowerSong Press, 2022. 93 pages. $16.00, paper.

Quarantine may seem like a vague dream to us now–a foggy memory of what once was, that confining thing that is seemingly far away. In an act of asserting the harrowing past, while solidifying the pandemic's long-lasting effects on socialization, Accardi brings us right back to those tumultuous times of solitude, fear, and uncertainty in her fifth poetry collection.

Readers may have forgotten how impactful COVID-19 was in 2020 when Accardi first began crafting these lyrical blips that summarize the nature of quarantine and the fear of illness, contagion, and isolation. Poems like "What We Call Time" emphasize the wish for normalcy. Amid the strong desire to touch each other, kiss each other, share drinks, and shake hands, the emphasis on cautious behavior forced people to experience intimacy elsewhere.

> … We wish away rights
> to handshakes, and
> watch old
> movies with longing,
> where couples kiss
> on the mouth …

This coping mechanism is not unfamiliar, and Accardi beautifully describes what forms of escapism we employed when we lost what was typically taken for granted: closeness.

Accardi tackles the ebbs and flows of quarantine with a consistent, blunt voice that errs on the side of a personal journal. Her repeated use of *and* and *so* feels natural, like the stuttering that occurred when we first had to speak in front of an in-person crowd after a year of Zoom meetings, or when we were at a loss for words after finally coming into physical contact with a relative who had been holed up in their house, awaiting vaccination. She begins multiple poems, such as "For Truth Would Be from a Line," "We Still Are Not Breathing," and "It's

Almost Dark" with the brave "And," as if picking up where she'd left off, breathlessly explaining society's demises and successes with an old friend she hasn't seen in a while.

Accardi analyzes the strange, desperate wants for closeness–such as sharing disease or plagues, like lice, as long as you are allowed to be around people–in her poem "I Told My Friend to Rub Her Lice Against my Hair."

> So I could get the comb through and deal with
> the nasty lotion and the sitting on a chair in front
> of the low kitchen sink so my mother would
> love me and fuss over my hair and touch
> my chin instead of being afraid as to what would happen.

The desperation for human contact spreads throughout years of Accardi's life as she connects the want for her mother's closeness even when she is infected with lice. The vast difference from then—a moment from her childhood—to now is that closeness was not an option when your loved ones were sick. Accardi makes us miss the way our mothers could cradle us, makes me wish I had been granted the chance to cradle my mother when she was ill during the pandemic. Her ability to attach the childish need to be taken care of to our new view on disease is moving, gently stroking the head of the reader: *Remember when?*

Though we may yearn to forget how isolating the peaks of COVID -19 were, Accardi allows the reader to experience those times again, with the same air of frustration and heartache, but also with the knowledge that things eventually got better—we eventually felt normal again. Accardi's most colorful thread connecting this poetry collection is that life is meant to be shared, no matter what comes next.

—*Molly Del Rossi*

Stories No One Hopes Are About Them by A. J. Bermudez. Iowa City, Iowa: University of Iowa Press, 2022. 144 pages. $17.50, paper.

A. J. Bermudez is a writer, filmmaker, and recipient of the Iowa Short Fiction Award for *Stories No One Hopes Are About Them*. The collection of short fictions has an expectation set in the title that dissolves in the narration by so many vibrant and witty voices who take the reins of the reader's experience. Each fiction contributes to a larger rhythm of contemporary life, bound together by pulses of power, exploitation, and identity. Bermudez makes the human experience feel animalistic and cruelly ironic, while simultaneously turning the mundane into something sacred and practiced.

Stories No One Hopes Are About Them was written for logophiles. Bermudez curated a veritable fauna of descriptive language that exists on the outskirts of my vernacular. The use of language is captivating with just enough obscure vocabulary to keep the reader prepared to consult their dictionary. Bermudez wields sensory details to carve out people, places, and events that linger on the psyche—navigating the broken fence between dark and hopeful comedy.

Bermudez combines existential wonder with sharp wit to develop protagonists in less-than-enviable positions. Each story grapples with virtuous elements of privilege, power, and circumstance to capture a mosaic of identities not limited by age, gender, sexuality, or culture. The author explores the psyche of her characters from the third-person perspective featuring the distinct voices of wise children, a dying doctor, and an execution singer named Eleanor:

> No one lectures Eleanor about psychology today.
> She sings a Verdi, a bit too jaunty for the occasion, but lovely nonetheless.
> She stays (she always stays) to watch the body crackle and jolt, the tautening of the veins beneath the paper-thin flesh of the throat, the scent of miscooked meat in the air.

It's through the psyche of these poor souls that the narrative occasionally prances with the disturbing and delusional. These dark undercurrents abbreviate humor and wholesomeness, capturing the human experience in three dimensions. Bermudez delivers her blows point blank, best summarized by the nightmare of a newly orphaned child named Helen:

> A faint, metronomic *drip … drip … drip …* escalates in volume as she rounds a corner. Ink drips into a small puddle at her feet. She raises the lantern.
> Above, framed by jagged shadows, are a slew of child-sized, skinned bodies, dangling from the ceiling like slabs of meat.
> Helen jolts awake.
> There are no bodies—none dead, at least—only a room full of sleeping children.

Though not every story is so macabre, Bermudez uses defamiliarization to punctuate tragedy with fascination, like the doomsday prepper eating leaves to prepare for a (potential) fall of man. Some characters, like the child named Ori, possess an infinite wisdom to be admired. Other characters captured in the snare of cruel irony, like the dying doctor Aman, could not be envied less:

> In his medical practice, Aman has often gently pressed the wound following the application of the final stitch, not to swab up the blood, but to reassure the patient. "There," he has often said. "That's the worst of it."
>
> He presses his own wound now, summoning the pain, wanting to live. This, he knows, in his rapidly hemorrhaging gut, is not the worst of it.
>
> He will miss the surgery in the morning ...

In my first impression of the title—*Stories No One Hopes Are About Them*—I presumed the fiction would focus on relatable people in unsavory scenarios. In hindsight, *Stories No One Hopes Are About Them* follows rather extraordinary people in tragically normal scenarios. Each fiction constellates a bright and sharp personality against a galaxy of banal evils, from racist microaggressions to war. Bermudez articulates human hypocrisy using bantering dialogue while stoking the flames of hope with inner monologue.

Stories No One Hopes Are About Them balances between half full and empty with something special for skeptics and hopefuls alike. It's difficult to synthesize any universal truths about the collection of shorts with its level of breadth and depth captured between the covers. These stories are best experienced by the reader firsthand because to dissect the cosmic joke would be to ruin it; and I doubt I would do it justice.

—*Sidney Miles*

I Walk Between the Raindrops by T.C. Boyle. New York, New York: Ecco, 2022. 288 pages. $28.99, cloth.

Still hammering away at the keyboard at age seventy-four, T.C. Boyle still maintains his place as America's grand poobah of literary fiction, particularly displaying his mastery in the short story genre; this most recent collection of thirteen tightly crafted slices of life intermixed with occasional forays into his beloved magical realism prove that he is still at the top of his game.

Possessing the investigative instincts of a homicide detective, Boyle so believably inhabits the psyches of his characters that you either commiserate with them or come to hate them. Take, for example, "The Shape of a Teardrop," where the narrators are a middle-aged woman and her thirty-one-year-old son who lives at home and has elevated mooching to an art form. Disgusted by his lack of contribution and his refusal to recognize his own child, her one and only grandchild, she sees no other option than to have him legally evicted. This is where the fun starts, because he countersues on the basis that it was her fault that he was even born and thus forced to endure the hardships of life. Both characters are deeply flawed, a Boyle specialty. The kid is an entitled millennial, so spoiled, self-absorbed, and lazy that you just want to punch him in the face, while the mother is so completely codependent that you want to slap her back to reality for being such an easy mark. The narrative switches back and forth from son to mother, and during the son's turn, he explains the court's ruling:

> But the judge was the judge and I was a minute speck on his docket, a blot, a nuisance, nothing. He set down his glasses, looked first to my parents, then to me, and pronounced his verdict. The case I cited, so he claimed, had been superseded by a more recent case and the weight thrown back on the parents' side, who had the absolute right to evict anybody from their own domicile, and in respect to that and his own determination in the case before him, he was finding against me and giving me forty-eight hours to vacate or face forcible eviction at the hands of the county sheriff who—and here he looked me right in the eye—really had better things to do. Understood?

Predictably, the kid waits until the last minute, forcing the county sheriff's department to send out an officer his own age to lay down the law before he begrudgingly moves, all the while resenting what he views as rude and unfair treatment, while the mother feels bad and wants to interfere, but her husband doesn't let her. The reader is left feeling little empathy for either of them because their beliefs and behavior causes each to reap what they have sown.

Boyle is a master of irony. In "The Apartment Set in France," an early-middle-aged man contracts with an older woman to pay a monthly fee for her apartment when she agrees to have it fall into his possession upon the event of her death. Little does the man realize that he is violation of the third of the three rules of real estate, which are the following: 1.) Location, location, location, 2.) Terms, terms, terms, and 3.) Never wait for an old lady to die. The agreement, entered into when the woman was 90, never does come to fruition as she becomes a 110-year-old supercentenarian, and then unbelievably turns 120.

In "SCS 750," the main character is determined to be a winner in the game of life by pushing his credit score over 700, the pursuit of which causes him to eventually turn his back on his best friend and a young woman who is physically out of his league when he comes to the realization that an association with their lower scores is holding him back. Why? Boyle explains:

> I was too young to remember a time before our leader became our leader, but I did have enough experience in my teens and now my early twenties to compare the way things were ten years ago and the way they are now. Which didn't make me a critic or rebel or anything even close—I was like anybody else, happy to live in a society where we could all prosper and love one another and work toward a common goal without worrying about getting ripped off or defrauded or attacked in a dark alley (actually, there are no dark alleys anymore, except in cop shows on TV, but you get the point). Regimes of the past may have used punishment as a way of enforcing laws and regulations, but the Social Credit Score program was more reward/reward, like vying for gold stars on your report card when you were a kid. It was self-regulating, that was the beauty of it, everybody doing everything they could to raise their score and avoid any hint of negativity. As our leader says, "Zima Credit insures that all roads are open to good citizens, while the bad ones have nowhere to turn."

In "What's Love Got to Do With It?" a middle-aged woman, who the reader can assume is attractive because she has a beautiful daughter, takes an Amtrak train from Los Angeles to Dallas to attend a business conference. On her journey she meets a young man named Eric, who is not especially good looking, somewhat unkempt bordering on being a slob, and has a huge chip on his shoulder towards pretty girls who won't give him the time of day. As the story unfolds we discover that he was friends with a campus shooter named E.R., who was enamored with one Mary Ellen Stovall, something of the campus queen. Eric, himself takes to stalking Stovall after an incident where she categorically rejects a clumsy pass that E.R. directs at her. He rationalizes he's doing it just to see what she's like, but she notices what he's doing, and he backs off. For E.R.'s part the humiliation he feels by her rejection turns to violence, and he guns down six students and wounds fourteen others before turning the gun on himself. Eric and the woman hit an impasse when he shows empathy for the shooter, and as the story develops he angrily reveals it is because he, too, is an involuntary virgin.

> "You have a daughter, right? Isn't that what you told me?"
> I nodded.
> "Is she pretty? She is, isn't she? Like Mary Ellen Stovall—pretty, right? Right?'"
> "I don't—I've never seen Mary Ellen Stovall, so how can I—?"
> "Would she go out with me? Would she have sex with me?"

After several rationalizations, none of which are especially realistic in light of how the world really works, the woman decides that honesty is the best policy: "No," I said. "No, she wouldn't.'"

That's life, and life isn't fair, so the rational are forced to play the cards they are dealt. At its core, this story reveals that Boyle is a realist and has a unique ability for forcing his readers to examine their stance on uncomfortable issues as well as themselves.

Kudos to T.C. Boyle. Most of our literary greats were spent, disillusioned, and unproductive by their mid-forties. But not Boyle. Going at the rate he is, he just might lap them.

—*John C. Krieg*

The World Keeps Ending, and the World Goes On by Franny Choi. New York, New York: Ecco, 2022. 144 pages. $27.99, paper.

In the new poetry collection, *The World Keeps Ending, and the World Goes On*, Franny Choi, an established queer, Korean American poet, frankly and intimately confronts the world's injustices towards marginalized peoples.

Using a creative apocalyptic lens, Choi imagines and reimagines the experiences of marginalized people of the past and present on both personal and universal scales. For example, in her poem "Prayer for the Untranslated Testimony," Choi recalls an experience that is, speculatively, her own, writing about how she witnessed the eerie sound of a boy in the night. She used this incident as a vehicle to communicate the many similar scenarios where people are in the position of testifying an experience, but those listening do not choose to hear or understand. One part that reflects the poem as a whole well states, "And some of my friends, I know, have names / that sound like this, like *I am here, I am here,* like / *why won't you answer,* like *why can't you see me.*" In other words, Choi uses a specific, personal experience that she had to connect readers to a larger issue at hand—the unheard voices and experiences of the marginalized.

Similarly, Choi includes a collection of four poems that are all titled the same: "Upon Learning That Some Korean War Refugees Used Partially Detonated Napalm Canisters as Cooking Fuel." Within this impressively experimental collection, Choi uses a situation she has not experienced directly herself (the experiences of Korean War refugees) to communicate the devastating injustices and hard life that refugees and other marginalized people experience.

One of the most engaging aspects of Choi's writing is her brilliant sense of intentionality. The specific way she organizes her book, the way each piece looks on the page, the pairings of words and sentences, and other details that seem miniscule are working together to communicate the complex themes and taboo subjects Choi intends. Choi organizes the book into five chapters. Though this seems like a common trend for poetry, she takes it a step further. She begins the whole book with a poem titled, "The World Keeps Ending, and the World Goes On," that works as an introduction to the content, a curtain slowly opening to show readers events that are about to take place. The last few lines of the poem state, "As everywhere, the apocalypse rumbled / the apocalypse remembered, our dear, beloved apocalypse—it drifted / slowly from the trees all around us, so loud we finally stopped hearing it." This introduction poem clearly defines the theme of the book—the idea that the world "ends" every day for marginalized people because of mistreatment that continues to permeate.

In terms of format and style, Choi presents readers with a perfect mix of hybridity and tradition. Readers can expect to flip through each page and find that each poem represents a sort of individuality. She uses physical line spacing and word positioning to add tension and bring focus to phrases or concepts. "Things That Already Go Past Borders" plays with alignment usesright alignment. "Comfort Poem" experiments with spacing in a way that forces readers' eyes to focus and notice certain words on the page more than others. It forces pauses instead of suggesting them.

As for content, Choi confidently communicates topics of a particularly taboo or stigmatized nature. For example, in her poem "Things That Already Go Past Borders," Choi confidently creates a list poem of things that go across borders to represent a particular scope towards the United States' immigration controversy. By juxtaposing materialistic, almost meaningless objects (like vegetables) with humans, Choi communicates the dehumanizing qualities and problematic characteristics behind certain anti-immigration opinions and laws.

Overall, Choi provides readers with a collection of poetry that loudly calls out the elephant in the room—that we are living amongst the ruins of an apocalypse of generations "so loud we finally stopped hearing it." In her poem "Science Fiction Poetry," she writes, "If we knew its name/ could we call it; if we called it would it come." By juxtaposing apocalyptic urgency and emergency with humanity's tendency to ignore uncomfortable realities regardless of their need for change, Choi gives readers an unforgettable collection.

—*Hailey Pedersen*

Maybe This Is What I Deserve by Tucker Leighty-Phillips. Ralston, Nebraska: Split/Lip Press, 2023. 47 pages. $12.00, paper.

Tucker Leighty-Phillips's story collection, *Maybe This Is What I Deserve*, showcases a variety of narrative constructions, techniques, and levels of complexity to embody multiple themes across multiple sets of stories with each one shedding a different type of light on their issues. Each story in the collection functions in a different way than the others yet remains connected to the others through the author's carefully crafted voice. Whether it's a public statement by a monster, a trip to Hollister, or death at a pool, each story leaves a vivid mark on the reader's mind, and even when most are only a page long, they beg to be read again.

Across the collection, Leighty-Phillips establishes powerful and recognizable themes through unfamiliar situations or by re-mystifying situations we know in a way that lets us see them with fresh eyes. In "Statement from the Silver-Taloned Monster Ravaging the Local Townspeople," the unfamiliar is explored through a public statement left on a bulletin board by a monster attacking and killing the townsfolk.

While the circumstances are unrecognizable as lived experiences, the situation remains viscerally real as the monster's words echo those of our own world. He "wants to assure the townspeople he hears their concerns," even as he kills them. His only remorse for the pain he inflicts is his brief statement: "*We're a community*, his statement reads, *and I see you. I'm listening.*" So even as the monster is unreal to our world, his words reflect the monsters at play in our own lives, pretending to care as they inflict immeasurable pain.

However, not all the stories handle the unreal. Some handle the real in ways that make it feel fantastic. Multiple stories in the collection function in this way such as "The Year We Stopped Counting," "Down the Tunnel, Up the Slide," and "The Hollister Store." "The Hollister Store" takes the situation of two kids hanging around the outside of a Hollister store, wondering what's inside and what exactly is so enthralling about the location to them. From the start, Leighty-Phillips refuses to let it just be a store. Instead, it is "like a party we hadn't been invited to join" or like a haunted house with fog billowing from the dark interior of the store. The location is elevated from store to spectacle in a way that defamiliarizes the location enough to see it as the children do: to see that poorly lit store with its different brands of clothes and wonder "what else could be imprinted on its heavy fabric." This ability to use the known to portray the unfamiliar and the unfamiliar to portray the known spans across the collection in an interesting back-and-forth of real and unreal.

Alongside these different manipulations of themes is a deft handling of language. Each story is carefully constructed and trimmed to focus completely on their individual themes. In particular, stories such as "The Whirlpool" and "Stages of Grief" show this masterful concentration of detail both in images and themes. While most stories in the collection are less than a page long and neither of these are the shortest stories in the book, both showcase Leighty-Phillips's craft in an exemplary manner. "The Whirlpool" unfolds over a brief paragraph, but its images of a young boy being sucked into a whirlpool are captured in captivating detail, such as "the ghostly choke of his tummy flab" and "the way his fingers pulled like telephone wire towards the ladder." Each line pulls the image into starker detail until its climactic close, fully realizing the image without a wasted word.

Meanwhile, "Stages of Grief," cowritten with Rachel Reeher, covers the five stages of grief: denial, anger, bargaining, depression, and acceptance, in concise fashion. In fewer than a dozen short lines, the stages are each covered over a fight between two siblings, one hitting the little brother and having to work through the stages before a parent can come punish the older sibling. The short form of the stories demands a level of skillful use of language that Leighty-Phillips rises to at each occasion no matter if the purpose is imagery or thematic value.

Each story is an impactful piece on its own. However, together they achieve an even greater effect. *Maybe This Is What I Deserve* captures each story without fail, with each bearing much more weight than its short form might suggest.

—*Sean Turlington*

***Jerks* by Sara Lippmann. New York, New York. Mason Jar Press, 2022. 154 pages. $21.00, paper.**

The decision to read Sara Lippmann's *Jerks* over Thanksgiving was not influenced by the fact the holiday would be spent surrounded by family and in desperation for a book that would both entertain me and communicate, *Leave me alone.* That was just coincidental. I read the first story while standing upright and walking to the living room, and as I crossed the threshold and took a seat, it hit me. These are all short stories about a bunch of jerks. The deeper I dove into the tales, the more I fell in love with each character: Lillian, Daphne, Brittany, and Skyler. As the reader progresses, understanding each character flaw and learning to love them despite it, the more they will be challenged to reason and respect their own character flaws.

"If You're Lucky, This Could Be You" takes us into the lush life of yoga and glamorized mental health where a new, graduate of rehab, Brit, invites her high-school-aged sister to attend a vinyasa class she is instructing at an overdone studio way out of Shania's price range. Shania, out of breath following the first flow, having decided to take it easy and modify the postures, hears her sister's voice ringing within her ear, "Try harder. If you are lucky, this could be you." Turning the page, I, too, needed to catch my breath and modify my posture, adjusting to the temperature of familial discomfort that Lippmann uses in writing to, I assume, get the heart pumping.

All stories showcase the imperfection, almost implicit, within the female body. The male characters are primarily misogynist, sex-driven, and content after being fed food and praise to their famished egos. Her line of sight traverses staple junk food, Jell-O containers and Coke, inconsiderate American tourists, creepy college friends, and the childish need to compete in some adults. "No Time for Losers" is a commentary on reality television and how it simply exploits the atrocities of the human experience. The main star, a wife performing household chores, enjoys "dosing up on reality TV" while completing mindless tasks. "It takes me out of myself," she says, flipping through episodes of suffering pregnant teenagers, hoarders, and family interventions.

Lippmann attacks humans for their shallow obsessions, their shameful journeys to find endorphins and dopamine. She takes the reader on mile-long runs, into fields of grass and wild orgies. There is blame to be found: constant creation of unnecessary drama and the need to see it manifested on screen if it is not happening before our eyes, in real time. Her language screams the fears we all embody, such as divorce, decay, and aloneness. It was in her stories that I finally saw these themes as simple manifestations of human nature, nothing more than good intentions.

It the dialogue where readers can locate the true manifestation and heart of the character's motive and personality. In her stories, the characters are seemingly normal, average, and like us in that they cater quite unapologetically to their desires; however, there is a line, and Lippmann crosses it every time in her storytelling. In every life circumstance and instance, there is unknown territory that stretches out beyond a world protected by assumption and decorum, but she beats down this wall of protection with a wooden bat and leads the reader to the other side. "Join me," she says. "This is where you have always wanted to go."

I once heard that being a jerk, or caring less what others think of you, can only result in a long-lasting and more fulfilling life. I wonder if that is true.

—*Emma J. Sullivan*

A Better Class of People by Robert Lopez. Ann Arbor, Michigan: Dzanc Books, 2022. 152 pages. $16.95, paper.

As a reader, I admit a bias toward setting. This is my primary means of connecting with a story. No sense of place, I preach to my students, and a reader will not feel grounded. It's a mantra I repeat often and a bias I own. Why, then, is it that I find Robert Lopez' *A Better Class of People*, a work almost entirely devoid of exterior setting, so captivating?

Rarely in this novel-told-in-stories are we fully shown the rooms, coffeehouses, or subway cars where the stories take place. Instead, we are invited inside the mind of the unnamed first-person narrator as he seeks meaning and truth in his memories and in the culture that surrounds him. Here Lopez employs a style that is fragmented and recursive, where time, imagination, and reality all merge. What we grow to understand is the narrator is in an institution where the residents are invited to share at meetings in order to "get better" and are occasionally rewarded with "furloughs." The narrator has been here "for as long as I can remember which is probably between two weeks and twelve years." He doesn't remember if he came here on his own or if someone else brought him. On furloughs, he uses his time to stand dangerously in traffic.

Through his memories and flashbacks, we learn about his past. He once had a career, working from inside a soul-crushing cubicle, pursued a woman named Esperanza, had a short-lived relationship with a woman named Django, and spent nights eating pie alone in a small apartment. There are remembered conversations on the topic of having children (a recuring theme) and encounters with a variety of characters with names like Watermelon Man, Roy-Boy, and his best friend Manny. He observes the people in the city, some of whom seem dead to him. On the subway, he watches a group of women smiling as they look at a baby across from them. We learn of his father's death by defenestration (the act of being thrown from a window), and his brother's accident that left him comatose. We learn little about his childhood, or his parents. ("I don't think I've told anyone about growing up," he says, "because it wasn't as bad as it sounds"). It is the accumulation of one's history that reveals their story, of course, and as the fragments of these narratives begin to coalesce, we are given a full sense of a character that is honest and heartbreaking. The mind is troubled, maybe traumatized, but not demented. The trouble stems largely from living in a culture imbued with violence, sometimes through the narrator's own imagined impulses, but more often related to his reflections on the news events around him.

In fact, as much as the narrative interiority reveals the individual character, it is the projection out, the mirror that forces us to look at the current state of the American psyche, that haunts most in this collection. As significant as his personal struggles are, the daily American news cycle and violence take equal toll. There are repeated references to real events, recognizable, though in slant. A reference to Flint, Michigan, for example: "This was also around the same time the drinking water went bad, according to the newspaper I found in the rubble of the old library. It started in one Michigan city and spread from there." And police brutality: "Sometimes the police would choke you to death instead of shooting you in the face. They did this if you called them on the phone for help or sold cigarettes or passed a counterfeit twenty at a convenience store." And the terrorist attacks of 9/11: "In my head he looks like the falling man from that photograph of the poor bastard who had to jump out of the towers as they burned." Set within the inner workings of the narrator's active mind, we are led to see anew the effects of the violence, images, and news that surround us.

I'm not sure *A Better Class of People* is intended as a postapocalyptic novel, but one cannot read the collection without considering postapocalyptic tropes. There has been an event, and the world is scattered, damaged. People are struggling to survive. The narrator is not sure if his family is still alive, or how he has ended up where he has. In the beginning is a man standing in traffic feeling the rush of passing cars, and in the end—as he draws stick figures in order to put the pieces of his story together—he is surrounded by the chaos of an active shooter event. In between we have a narrator who lives in a tormented, fragmented world. It turns out that the novel is not devoid of setting after all. Instead, it is a world that is all too familiar. *A Better Class of People* is a sad, beautiful book that says much about our current state, in a voice that is stunning.

—*Daryl Farmer*

Admit This to No One by Leslie Pietrzyk. Los Angeles, California: The Unnamed Press, 2023. 258 pages. $18.00, paper.

Leslie Pietrzyk masterfully weaves fourteen stories together in *Admit This to No One*. She creates a constant blend of perspective with each chapter that leaves the reader trying to figure out which characters are being put under the microscope at any given moment.

The life of a politician is rarely mess free, and the Speaker's is no different. This collection of stories largely shed light on the Speaker of the House and several people who have close relations with him: a daughter from his first marriage, a daughter from his third marriage, his right-hand woman at the office, and so on—though there are a few random perspectives that are sprinkled in to keep readers on their toes.

It feels as if the reader is constantly being transported into a new mind. Pietrzyk provides extensive inner monologues that reveal her characters' most private thoughts in an extremely realistic way as the sentences almost run together. At the end of the first story, "'Til Death Do Us Part," we see Madison have dinner with her father, the Speaker—but only because court-mandated visits were part of the divorce settlements. The story ends (temporarily) with a "religious nut" trying to knife the Speaker because of his atheist beliefs and surprisingly to everyone involved, but most of all Madison herself, she throws herself in front of her father to save his life:

> I'm not screaming or going "look out, look out, look out" because I'm plunged underwater, off a bridge, into that bad dream where you can't move, chest crushed into a deflated ball and legs heavy like the sandbags I helped pile down by the waterfront when that hurricane blew up from the Outer Banks a million years ago and basements and stores flooded in Old Town and there are all these thoughts, and I can't decide if I love my father and I do, I have to, because he's the only father I'll ever have, and when my father stands up, and the shadows are pushing and shoving, and the bad-luck waiter comes barreling in, tackling the shadows, and everyone's screaming their heads off now, even me, and I jump up and fling myself on top of my father's body, crashing him to the hard floor, protecting his chest— protecting him—and the knife slides carefully into my body, like I'm butter, "like I'm butter," is exactly what I think I'll tell the cops and TV people, and it doesn't hurt, nothing hurts right now, and I feel brave and also so stupid, and I'll tell that to the cops too, tell everyone because that's who will be listening to me, everyone, and I will tell them, *This is what love looks like, right?*

All of the stories explore traditionally "uncomfortable" topics. Characters deal with racism, gender roles, wealth divides, discrimination, politics, the list goes on. One of the stories discussing race is "Green in Judgment," where Christine encounters a Black woman and her son who are checking out in front of Christine and having issues with coupons. The story concludes with Christine recounting this story at her workplace:

> She [Christine] notices herself glancing around the room to see if the Black employees are in yet, and when she notices herself noticing this she understands—or imagines she does—exactly what she has done.

Names are like currency throughout the text. Typically you know the main characters' names are known, though the Speaker is only ever referred to as the Speaker, I think to make him a little less human. But there are often names omitted by supporting characters. In the case of "I Believe in Mary Worth," Mary-Grace's character is referred to as "She-Beast," and then her name is revealed halfway through the chapter. In following chapters including her, the names are used interchangeably.

While not all stories are directly related to the Speaker, I was often left wondering if the seemingly randomized stories were somehow related after all and Pietrzyk simply didn't feel the need to tell us.

There is a colorful variety of perspective provided by a range of different people that the audience is meant to piece together on their own. This brings an element that draws the reader closer to the stories, because close attention is needed to make the many connections among stories. I truly think that *Admit This to No One* shows that—for all of us—there is more than meets the eye. There are layers upon layers that make us human and contribute to our human experience. By stringing these fourteen stories together, Pietrzyk displays human connection and provides a space for us to understand life from different view-points.

—*Olivia Fowler*

Animal, Roadkill, Ashes, Gone by **Emily Pittinos. Durham, North Carolina: Bull City Press, 2022. 58 pages. $12.95, paper.**

Some books need to be written. Some stories need to be given a due space. In *Animal, Roadkill, Ashes, Gone*, Emily Pittinos creates such a space for the story of her father's sudden passing. Like the cannisters of his ashes that accompany her and the man she calls Boyfriend to Pictured Rocks National Lakeshore, four essays encapsulate her grief encounters after her father is gone. "He daydreamed of jumping off the rocks there—," she says of her father as she takes her reader on an exertion from lower Michigan to upper on his behalf a year after the funeral, weaving her grief, in its nonlinear expression, through other journeys across country and memory and visitations of death's finality.

"Imagine," Pittinos says in the first essay "Prey Animal," "a bird dying of fear in your hands." This is where we begin: with a bird. A fragile body that can be scared, literally, to death, in the hands of a caretaker because it is panic stricken, unable to wing free.

The body—the animal body—is vulnerable, Pittinos demonstrates. Her father's ribs break when he falls on black ice. Next, liver failure. Next, a stomach bleed. Next, a phone call in the essay "Gone" telling Pittonos that her father has become the panic-stricken bird suddenly released from his embodied home, and she too, then, becomes a panic-stricken bird curling into a heap on the ground before the World War II Memorial in DC as if in a display of "patriotism before all the monument's lost, anonymous lives."

Grief is followed by guilt. "Take your trip," her father had told her, "I'll be here when you get back." So, she drove with a college roommate across several states not knowing this was the last time she'd see him alive.

Driving, once again, across several states in a different direction, she memorializes her pain with flowers picked along roadsides, and sex, meandering from Joshua Tree to Jackson Hole and back to Michigan, with Boyfriend, toward her father's unrealized dream. "[W]e stumbled onto Mosquito Beach," she says in "Ashes," referring to an inlet along Lake Superior's shoreline at Pictured Rocks. "It would've been a picturesque moment to scatter my dad's ashes, if I hadn't left them in the car …." She adds," I didn't quite forget my dad's remains in the car; I also didn't quite make the choice to leave him behind."

And this impulse, dear reader, is something I understand—two tablespoons full of my mother's ashes, a year after her funeral, still in a small velvet blue bag waiting for their final resting place. It's difficult to make the choice of leaving them anywhere that seems "far too lonely." "Once we left," says Pittinos, "a piece of him would be stranded, alone, on a strange beach, mixing and eroding with the sand for eternity."

She had done this once before—left her father behind. She couldn't do it again.

Or again, in her memories. "When my father first died," she says in "Roadkill," "I was paralyzed by the fear of forgetting him." Paralyzed, nearly shocked toward her own bewildered ending. "For a while, it seemed like there were dead animals in every shadow in my neighborhood … the sidewalk felt littered with dead sparrows, ants crawling out of their eyes." Death doesn't come naturally to our psyche. The body troubles itself to grieve and grieve well if such an achievement is possible.

It isn't. "When it is unlikely that a bird could be released into the wild and reclaim its natural abilities to survive," Pittinos informs us in "Prey Animal," "it is considered more humane to euthanize."

In four essays, Pittonis considers her potential for this—the seizure of grief and guilt taking breath away until she can accept the "practice of moving [her] father aside." It feels like a "slim horror," embracing this ritual of letting go to keep going. But she does it. "[L]oved ones will die," she tells us in "Ashes, "and it can happen at any time." Hoping her own bird body will survive, she holds it in these essays, feeling the certainty of death in her very skin, examining, as she says in "Roadkill," her own "signs of life."

—*Kimberly Ann Priest*

***Girl County* by Jacqueline Vogtman. Ann Arbor, Michigan: Dzanc Books, 2023. 187 pages. $16.95, paper.**

Each story in Jacqueline Vogtman's *Girl County* feels like being pushed into an oil painting and getting lost in each stroke. Each ending rips the reader from the canvas, leaving them to stare at the art they just experienced. The worlds Vogtman creates range from magical to disturbing, and she's not afraid to mix the two. Whether its set in a dystopia or early twentieth-century Scotland, Vogtman invites the reader to experience her stories fully, tethered by compelling protagonists that embody the struggles of what it means to be human.

Vogtman contrasts human struggle with supernatural elements. In "BI6FOOT," the protagonist searches for the famed mythical beast and struggled to maintain her belief in the creature. All the while, the protagonist relives moments in her life when her belief in herself and her innocence is shaken, usually by outside forces:

> I hated confession. Why did I have to tell my secrets to a stranger, who proceeded to scold me for them? Like the time I told the priest my neighbor had asked to look down my underpants the summer before I turned eleven, and since I pulled them down myself I suspected it must have been my fault, and the priest confirmed my suspicion. Still, I believed back then.

Relatably, irritably, the protagonist is constantly invalidated. This is where Vogtman digs deep into the dirt on what it feels like to not just be human, but specifically a woman, and she hits gold. The reader can understand the protagonist and each of her decisions, even if the reader might not make the same one. The protagonist is not perfect. She's riddled with flaws and insecurities, which make her all that much more relatable, and it hurts so much worse when they're thrown back at her to invalidate her thoughts and emotions. She is continuously burdened with guilt from putting herself in potentially harmful situations to alleviate the responsibility of those who abused her. The protagonist's search for bigfoot concurrent with her search for validation of her emotions and belief that culpability is on her abusers, not her, is beautifully crafted and makes the reader wonder if finding bigfoot will be easier than finding the validation she craves.

As previously stated, Vogtman's world building is masterful. Her most compelling setting may be in "Girl County," although, the disturbing and isolating setting of "Jubilee Year" and its inclusion of themes of sisterhood, love, and bodily autonomy is also a strong contender. Still, "Girl County" begs the reader to keep reading between the lines. Set in a dystopian future in which everyone drinks milk and most everyone is dead or dying, "Girl County" focuses on a rather mundane character: a farmer named Noah. Noah doesn't have any particularly lofty goals. It seems he's content to just survive, until he comes across a strange girl who can barely talk. Vogtman weaves a heartwarming story about a man providing for his new surrogate daughter and even includes family Christmas, but there's no escaping the feeling of spiders crawling up the spine, the unwanted knowledge that something is deeply wrong. The world continues to expand with each word, continually unfolding more and more disturbing facets of its society, resulting in a dramatic conclusion that will situate itself firmly in the forefront of the reader's mind whether they want it to or not.

"Girl County" is not for the faint of heart. It uniquely explores gender and class, making sure not to pull any punches. Come for the found family trope, stay for the social commentary, and be thoroughly horrified by much of the imagery. In other words, Vogtman starts off her story collection with a bang. The reader may find themselves having to stop after reading "Girl County" to digest, but that's needed for pretty much every story.

Read, sit, think is how I best recommend reading *Girl County*. These stories have a way of haunting the reader. They don't dissipate like breath in cold air. They hang around like a ghost. *Girl County* is not an ephemeral form of entertainment. It puts the reader in conversation with its themes and warrants extra time to sit with its stories. With impressively fleshed-out worlds, characters, and themes, each ending feels like flipping on a light switch after sitting for hours in a dark room. Blink. Let the eyes readjust. Then dive into Vogtman's next world full of humanity, horror, and hope.

—*Mar Prax*

Book of Gods and Grudges by Jessica L. Walsh. Glenview, Illinois: Glass Lyre Press, 2022. 81 pages. $16.00, paper.

"It is a comfort," claims the speaker in Jessica L. Walsh's *Book of Gods and Grudges*, "to know our god grieves / when we die."

And comfort, I think, is what this speaker has come to know through groans. Human groaning. The harsh realities of upper Midwestern living, aging and age, the hard usefulness and tender uselessness of the body, choosing smartly despite all passions, and a quest toward forgiveness that, she says in "All Her Bones Are Scattered," drains the "bones of marrow"—all of which I, also, an upper Midwesterner, know well. We are small, says Walsh in "In Human Years," "young / and then gone." "We are replaceable / to the divine / We are replaced." There is comfort. There is no comfort. This is how we live and who we are.

"[G]rudges," says this starkly honest speaker in "When My Daughter Tells Me I Was Never Punk," are what "I made my life out of ... when I saw the odds placed against me." And this speaker makes no secret of those odds—sickness, alcoholism, poverty. In waiting rooms, with scratch-offs, from a lineage of "blade, hymn, tale" in "No Tree for Shade," Walsh's speaker understands her existence is not simple nor simplistic. She is, body and soul, party, and parcel of men and women who have been wronged and done wrong, who, as she says in this same poem, "went to church with knives / in their boots, bodices, sleeves"

Admitting her woes and wounds with an integrity that both damns her and makes her a vestibule of grace, this woman is grateful for the quiet toughness of her people bitterly surviving against the elements in ways that also make them intolerable—herself, too. "My first found kin were killers," she says in "Trespasses." "On the Pere Marquette," she relishes the rhythms of fisherman and fish out on the lake where she has come to escape this whole cast of characters, present and past, but not to leave them—only to need them again, to "go back."

To this speaker, our quest for comfort—relational, material, physical—is normal but already thwarted. "Earth's slightly non-spherical," she explains in "Contaminated," "its poles a little akimbo." Efforts toward perfection are futile. In that same poem, she sits with a woman crying and does not leave her when the woman pours out faith that President Donald Trump will make her world right again, the centers of their two universes tilting away. She, in that moment, doesn't cherry-pick, instead holding the woman's hand through political sting. "[A]nd I would hold it again," she says to her reader "If I lose you here I lose you."

"As a child," she tells us in "Reliquary," as premise, "I saw no border between wild and blade— / holy both." Her husband's cancer, grandmother's death, and the "recovery" that, in "Like the Last Ice of Spring," shrinks her "into [a] thick waisted woman / who jumps at small noises / and shakes at small changes," have wizened her beyond shallow positivity and easy solutions. What remains in adulthood is, once again, the wildness of a broken bird and prayer as it twitches and dies in "The Year of Confirmation," as well as the blade of her mother's hand scooping it up with swift practicality, plopping it into a bag, and walking slowly to the trash can.

Book of Gods and Grudges doesn't romanticize. There is only life in the body as is, and this body is both friend and enemy. In one of my favorite poems, "Call It Self Care," she states, "My therapist is forgetting maybe everything, surely me. / Today she forgets my daughter, then places her in college. / Gently I walk her back, watching her strain to know / what she knows …." And then, a bit later in the poem, "I tell her I'm feeling better. I am not." Returning to her old patterns of worry and worry for others—the very habits she came to a therapist to change—she admits, "When my benefits run out for the year, I come anyway / worried that others will leave her, that she needs me." Their mutual humanity lingers between them. No deity, religion, or spiritual practice rescues either from her personal fragilities. Both therapist and patient live here, in the earthly realm, where even the existence of this book of poems testifies, as the speaker says in "A Scale of Weed to Vine," that one must "keep a poem going to stay alive."

In *Gods and Grudges*, those of us who grew up in the unforgiving upper Midwest know what it means to "hurt enough / to carry a Bible, / download self-help podcasts," try yoga, and dream of sabbatical, just like the speaker in "Must Be Nice." None of these devices alleviate anger, prayer, wasp stings, broken birds, the lake all remain. We live here with all of it. But, more than this, we know that we come from people for whom "burnout is a luxury." So, we don't burn out. "*Do you really think you can fall apart?*" the speaker imagines her parents asking when she considers telling them she feels like falling apart. "*People like us—we don't.*" We don't. "It is a comfort," says Walsh in "In Human Years," "to know our god grieves / when we die." In fact, for us, it might be the only comfort there is.

—*Kimberly Ann Priest*

Contributors' Notes

Sally Ashton is a writer, teacher, and editor-in-chief of *DMQ Review*, an online journal featuring poetry and art. Author of four books, Ashton's most recent work, *The Behaviour of Clocks*, a hybrid series, was published in 2019 by WordFarm Press. Her recent work appears in *Orion Press*, *Los Angeles Review of Books*, *Oakland Arts Review*, *SALT Press*, and *Axon Journal* (Australia).

Michael Beard studies poetry in the master of fine arts program at Bowling Green State University. His poems have appeared or are forthcoming in *The Mantle Poetry*, *Thin Air Magazine*, *Oakland Arts Review*, and the 2021 Southern Literary Festival Anthology, among other places.

Rebecca Bernard is an assistant professor of creative writing at Angelo State University and serves as a fiction editor for *The Boiler*. Her work has appeared or is forthcoming in *Shenandoah*, *Southwest Review*, *Colorado Review*, and *North American Review*, among other journals. Her debut collection of stories won the 2021 Non/Fiction Collection Prize held by *The Journal* and was published by Mad Creek Books in 2022.

Marin Bodakov was born on April 28th, 1971, in Veliko Tarnovo, Bulgaria. He holds a degree in Bulgarian philology from St. Kliment Ohridski University in Sofia. He teaches at St. Kliment Ohridski University, and since 2000, he has managed the literary department of Kultura newspaper. He is the author of five books of poetry, most recently *Naïve Art* (2011), for which he received the Ivan Nikolov National Literary Award.

Megan Borocki has an MFA in poetry from Bowling Green State University and serves as poetry editor for *Mid-American Review*. Their work has recently appeared in *Olney* and *The Hunger*, with work forthcoming in *Landlocked*.

Margaret Emma Brandl is the author of the novella *Tuscaloosa (Or, In April, Harpies)*. Other writing has appeared in journals such as *Gulf Coast*, *The Cincinnati Review*, *Yalobusha Review*, *Pithead Chapel*, and *Cheap Pop*. She earned her doctorate at Texas Tech University and her MFA at Notre Dame, and she teaches at Austin College.

Kathryn Bratt-Pfotenhauer's work has previously been published or is forthcoming in *Cherry Tree, Beloit Poetry Journal, Meridian*, and others. A 2023 Pushcart Prize winner, they have received support from *The Seventh Wave* and *Tin House*, won awards from the Ledbury Poetry Festival and Bryn Mawr College, and were a finalist in the Munster Literature Centre's 2021 International Chapbook Competition. Their chapbook, *Small Geometries*, is being published with Ethel Zine & Micro Press in 2023. They attend Syracuse University's MFA program.

Clara Burghelea is a Romanian-born poet with an MFA in poetry from Adelphi University. Her poems and translations appeared in *Ambit, Waxwing, The Cortland Review*, and elsewhere. Her second poetry collection, *Praise the Unburied*, was published in 2021 with Chaffinch Press. She is the reviews editor of *Ezra, An Online Journal of Translation*.

Alyx Chandler (she/her) is a writer from the South who received her MFA in poetry at the University of Montana, where she taught composition and poetry. She is a publicist for *Poetry Northwest*, a reader for *Electric Literature*, and former poetry editor for *CutBank*. Her poetry can be found or is forthcoming in *Cordella Magazine, Greensboro Review, SWWIM, Anatolios Magazine, Sweet Tree Review*, and elsewhere.

Abigail Chang is a writer based in Taipei, Taiwan. Her work appears or is forthcoming at *Gone Lawn, Gulf Stream, Parentheses Journal*, and elsewhere.

Clayton Adam Clark lives in St. Louis, his hometown, where he works as a public health researcher and mental health counselor. *A Finitude of Skin*, published by Moon City Press in 2018, was his debut collection. In addition to Moon City Review, his individual poems have recently appeared in *Shenandoah, Salamander, Portland Review*, and elsewhere.

Zoa Coudret is a genderqueer fiction writer and poet. Their work has appeared in *Peach Mag, New South, Longleaf Review, The Lumiere Review, The Hallowzine*, and elsewhere. They are a graduate student in fiction at Northern Michigan University and work as an associate editor for *Passages North*.

Molly Del Rossi is a student at Missouri State University in Springfield, Missouri. She has been published in *LOGOS: A Journal of Undergraduate Research* and was a finalist in the 2021 MSU Student Poetry Competition for Moon City Press.

Darren Demaree is the author of seventeen poetry collections, most recently *clawing at the grounded moon* (April Gloaming, 2022). He is editor-in-chief of the *Best of the Net Anthology* and managing editor of *Ovenbird Poetry*.

Aran Donovan lives in Virginia. Her work has appeared in *Best New Poets* and is forthcoming in *Willow Springs* and *Zone 3*.

Janelle Drumwright is the production editor at *Carve Magazine* and teaches creative writing workshops at the Writers Studio. Her work has appeared in *Necessary Fiction, Mulberry Fork Review,* and *Naugatuck River Review*. In her free time, she volunteers as a mentor for incarcerated writers.

Daryl Farmer is the author of *Bicycling Beyond the Divide* (Bison Books, 2012), a nonfiction book that chronicles a bicycle ride across the western United States, and *Where We Land* (Brighthorse Books, 2016), a collection of short fiction. Recent work has appeared in *Terrain. org, Ploughshares,* and *Natural Bridge*. He is an associate professor at the University of Alaska-Fairbanks.

Sandra Fees has been published in *SWWIM, River Heron Review, Orange Blossom Review,* and *Harbor Review*. She was longlisted for the 2021 Frontier Open Prize, a finalist for *Witness'* 2022 Literary Awards, and a semi-finalist for *Nimrod*'s 2021 Pablo Neruda Prize for Poetry. She is a former Berks County, Pennsylvania, poet laureate and author of *The Temporary Vase of Hands* (Finishing Line Press, 2017).

Amy Fleury is the author of two collections of poems, *Beautiful Trouble* (2004) and *Sympathetic Magic* (2013), both from Southern Illinois University Press, and a chapbook, *Reliquaries of the Lesser Saints* (RopeWalk Press, 2010). Recent poems have appeared in *Image, 32 Poems, Crazyhorse,* and *Los Angeles Review,* among others.

Sherrie Flick is the author of the novel *Reconsidering Happiness* (University of Nebraska Press, 2009) and two short story collections, *Thank Your Lucky Stars* (2018) and *Whiskey, Etc.* (2016), both with Autumn House Press. Recent work has appeared in *Ploughshares, New England Review,* and *Booth*. She's a senior editor at *SmokeLong Quarterly*, served as a series editor for *The Best Small Fictions 2018*, and is co-editor for *Flash Fiction American* (W.W. Norton, 2023).

Olivia Fowler is a graduate student and freelance editor. She received her bachelor's degree in professional and technical writing from

Missouri State University and is pursuing her master's degree in the same subject from her alma mater.

Harrison Gatlin lives in Brooklyn, New York, where he works as a copywriter. He received his MFA from the University of Alabama in 2022 and has pieces in *The Missouri Review* and *Coastal Shelf,* among others.

Kate Gehan's debut short story collection, *The Girl & The Fox Pirate,* was published by Mojave River Press in 2018. Her writing has appeared in *SmokeLong Quarterly, McSweeney's Internet Tendency, Split Lip Magazine, People Holding, Literary Mama,* and *Cheap Pop,* among others. She is a nonfiction editor at *Pithead Chapel.*

Rich Glinnen, a Best of the Net nominee, lives in Bayside, New York. His work can be read in various print and online journals.

Susanna Goldfinger is a writer and cartoonist based in New York City.

Melissa Goodnight's work has appeared *in Mud Season Review, Lunch Ticket,* and *Litro,* among others. She earned her BA from Missouri State University, her MA in Creative Writing from the University of North Carolina at Charlotte, and her MFA from Mississippi University for Women. She lives in Atlanta.

Matthew Guenette's forthcoming book of poems is *Doom Scroll* (University of Akron Press, 2023). His previous collections are *Vasectomania* (University of Akron Press, 2017), *American Busboy* (University of Akron Press, 2011), and *Sudden Anthem* (Dream Horse Press, 2008). He lives in Wisconsin with his wife, their two kids, and a 20-pound cat named Butternut.

Sara Henning is the author of *View from True North,* co-winner of the 2017 Crab Orchard Series in Poetry Open Competition Award and the 2019 High Plains Book Award. Her latest collection of poems, *Terra Incognita,* won the 2021 Hollis Summers Poetry Prize and will be released by Ohio University Press in March 2022. Her honors include the Lynda Hull Memorial Poetry Prize, the George Bogin Memorial Award, the Allen Ginsberg Poetry Award, and awards from the Sewanee Writers' Conference and the Vermont Studio Center. She is an assistant professor of English at Marshall University.

Ric Hoeben is an American fiction and creative nonfiction writer whose work is most often set in the American South. Hoeben resides in Georgetown, South Carolina, and is a Native American activist for the

Chicora under his tribal name, "Kid Ric." He attended the University of Florida for his MFA in fiction. Hoeben's most recent work appears in *Tampa Review, storySouth, Glimmer Train*, and others.

Susan Holcomb holds an MFA in writing from the Vermont College of Fine Arts. Her writing has been or will soon be published in *Southern Indiana Review, The Boston Globe, Crab Creek Review*, and elsewhere.

Vladislav Hristov was born in 1976 in Shumen, Bulgaria. He holds a doctorate in plant breeding, works as a journalist, and is the author of six poetry books. Hristov's haiku were selected for inclusion in the educational text *Earth in Sunrise* by Richard Gilbert and David Ostman (Red Moon Press, 2017). He resides in Plovdiv, Bulgaria.

Shen Chen Hsieh is an illustrator, instructor, and art director in Missouri. She studied and graduated with an MFA in the Visual Study program at Missouri State University. She currently works as an art director in the local design industry.

Blake Johnson holds an MFA in writing from the Vermont College of Fine Arts. His writing has been or will soon be published in *Southern Indiana Review, The Boston Globe, Crab Creek Review*, and elsewhere.

Robert P. Kaye's flash stories have appeared in *SmokeLong Quarterly, Hobart, Penn Review, Fiction Southeast, Juked*, and elsewhere. He hosts the Works In Progress open mic at Hugo House in Seattle and is an editor with *Pacifica Literary Review*.

Shane Kowalski has an MFA in fiction from Cornell University. His first book of short fiction, *Small Moods*, was recently published by Future Tense Books in 2022.

John C. Krieg describes himself as a former landscape architect, swimming pool contractor, and outlaw pot farmer.

Kathryn Kulpa has stories in *Atticus Review, Five South, Flash Frog, Pithead Chapel, SmokeLong Quarterly*, and other journals. Her work has been chosen for *Best Microfiction 2022* and *Wigleaf*'s 2022 Longlist. Her flash chapbook, *Cooking Tips for the Demon-Haunted*, is forthcoming in 2023 from *New Rivers Press*.

Anna Leahy's latest books are the poetry collections *Gloss, What Happened Was:*, and *Aperture* and the nonfiction book *Tumor*. Her essays have won top awards from *Mississippi Review, Los Angeles Review, Ninth Letter*, and *Dogwood*. She edits the international *Tab Journal* and has been a fellow at MacDowell and the American Library in Paris.

DS Levy lives in the Midwest. Her fiction has been nominated for the Pushcart Prize and *JMWW*'s *Best Microfiction* and was included in the *Wigleaf Top 50 Very Short Fictions*.

Emily Lowe is an MFA candidate in nonfiction at the University of North Carolina Wilmington, where she is the fiction coeditor of *Ecotone Magazine*.

Ma Hua was born in Tianjin, China, in 1972 and graduated from Fudan University. He started writing poetry and plays at the university and was a core member of Fudan Poetry Club and the head of Yanyuan Theatre Club. In 2004, he passed away in a car accident while volunteering as a village teacher in Yunnan.

Angie Macri's recent work appears in *Bennington Review*, *The Journal*, and *Sixth Finch*. Macri is an adjunct professor in the English Department at Hendrix College in Conway, Arkansas.

Stefan Manasia is a Romanian poet and journalist and an editor of *Tribuna* cultural magazine. He founded Thoreau's Nephew Reading Club in Cluj, which became the largest Romanian-Hungarian literary community in Transylvania. He published six volumes of poetry and had his poems translated in Hungarian, French, German, Polish, and Hebrew. He is also the author of a collection of essays and literary chronicles called *The Aroma Stabilizer* (Editura Tribuna, 2016) and a short story collection, *The Chronovisor* (Polirom, 2020).

Skyler Melnick is an MFA candidate for fiction at Columbia University. Her writing has appeared in *Night Picnic*, *Palaver Arts Magazine*, and *The Catalyst*, and she received the University of Southern California's Edward W. Moses Undergraduate Creative Writing Prize in 2021.

Sidney Miles is a writer and graduate student at Missouri State University.

Nancy Carol Moody is the author of two collections of poetry, *The House of Nobody Home* (FutureCycle Press, 2016) and *Photograph with Girls* (Traprock Books, 2009), as well as a chapbook, *Mermaid* (Tiger's Eye Press, 2016). She has had poetry appear in *Moon City Review*, *The Gettysburg Review*, *The Southern Review*, *Tampa Review*, and *Nimrod*.

Laura Leigh Morris is the author of *Jaws of Life* (West Virginia University Press, 2018), a short story collection, and *The Stone Catchers*, a novel, forthcoming from the University Press of Kentucky. "The Pantry Store" is an excerpt from *The Stone Catchers*.

Mark Neely is the author of the poetry collections *Beasts of the Hill* (2012) and *Dirty Bomb* (2015), both published by Oberlin College Press. His third collection, *Ticker*, won the Idaho Prize for Poetry and was published by Lost Horse Press in 2021. He has also been awarded an NEA Poetry Fellowship, an Indiana Individual Artist grant, the *Field* Poetry Prize, and the Concrete Wolf Chapbook Award. He is a professor of English at Ball State University and a senior editor at *River Teeth: A Journal of Nonfiction Narrative*.

Shawn Nocher is the author of *A Hand to Hold in Deep Water* (2021) and *The Precious Jules* (2022), both published by Blackstone Publishing. She teaches master's-level writing courses at Johns Hopkins University and lives in Baltimore, Maryland, with her husband.

Jamie Odeneal is a writer and teacher living in the Washington, DC, area. Her work has appeared in *Los Angeles Review of Books*, the *Furious Gravity* anthology, and *Bull* and is forthcoming in *Meetinghouse Magazine*.

Suphil Lee Park is the author of the poetry collection *Present Tense Complex*, winner of the Marystina Santiestevan Prize (Conduit Books & Ephemera, 2021), and a poetry chapbook, *Still Life*, selected by Ilya Kaminsky as the winner of the 2022 Tomaž Šalamun Prize, forthcoming from Factory Hollow Press. She has received fiction prizes from *Indiana Review* and *Writer's Digest*.

Hailey Pedersen is pursuing a graduate degree in creative writing at Missouri State University, where she serves on the staff of Moon City Press and *Moon City Review*.

Matthias Politycki is a bestselling author and is ranked amongst the most successful contemporary literary German authors.

Mar Prax was born and raised in Valdez, Alaska, and is pursuing an undergraduate creative writing degree at Missouri State University. She won the Fiction Open to the Public category in the 39th Annual Statewide UAA/*Anchorage Daily News* Creative Writing Contest, and her work is featured in *LitSite Alaska*.

Bryan D. Price is the author of the forthcoming collection *A Plea for Secular Gods: Elegies* (What Books Press, 2023). His work is forthcoming or has appeared in *UCity Review, Crab Creek Review,* and *RHINO Poetry,* among others. He lives in San Diego.

Kimberly Ann Priest is the author of *Slaughter the One Bird* (Sundress Publications, 2021), finalist for the American Best Book Awards, and chapbooks *The Optimist Shelters in Place* (Small Harbor Publishing, 2022), *Parrot Flower* (Glass Poetry Press, 2021), and *Still Life* (PANK Books, 2021). She is an associate poetry editor for *Nimrod International Journal of Prose and Poetry* and an assistant professor at Michigan State University.

Sharmin Rahman is a writer living in Los Angeles. She was born in Bangladesh and raised in Brooklyn. She graduated from Boston University and the UCLA Writers' Program.

Michael Rogner is a restoration ecologist living in northern California. His poetry has appeared in *Willow Springs Magazine, The Los Angeles Review, the minnesota review, Barrow Street,* and elsewhere.

Luke Rolfes' first book, *Flyover Country* (2015), won the Georgetown Review Short Story Collection Contest, and his second book, *Impossible Naked Life* (2022), won the Acacia Fiction Prize from Kallisto Gaia Press. He is an assistant professor of creative writing at Northwest Missouri State University, edits *The Laurel Review,* and has served as a mentor in the AWP Writer to Writer Mentorship Program.

Leigh Camacho Rourks is a Cuban-American author living and working in central Florida, where she is an assistant professor at Beacon College. She won the St. Lawrence Book Award for her debut story collection, *Moon Trees and Other Orphans* (2019), which received a starred review from Kirkus Reviews. She is also the recipient of the Glenna Luschei Prairie Schooner Award and the Robert Watson Literary Review Prize. She is the co-author of *Digital Voices: Podcasting in the Creative Writing Classroom* (2023) from Bloomsbury Academic.

Matt Rowan lives in Los Angeles. He edits *Untoward* and is author of the collections *How the Moon Works* (Cobalt Press, 2021), *Big Venerable* (CCLaP Publishing, 2015), and *Why God Why* (Love Symbol Press, 2013). His work has appeared or is forthcoming in *Split Lip Magazine, Electric Literature, SmokeLong Quarterly,* and *Necessary Fiction,* among others.

Adam Scheffler received his MFA in poetry from the Iowa Writers' Workshop and his PhD in English from Harvard. His first book of poems, *A Dog's Life,* was the winner of the Jacar Press Poetry Book Contest, and his second, *Heartworm,* was just released by Moon City

Press as the winner of its Moon City Poetry Award. He teaches in the Harvard College Writing Program.

Teo Shannon is a queer, Latinx poet. He holds an MFA from Pacific University and is pursuing his doctorate at the University of Nebraska-Lincoln. He is a co-founder and co-editor-in-chief of *Cotton Xenomorph*.

Martha E. Snell's poetry appears in journals such as *Ninth Letter*, *Moon City Review*, *Cutthroat*, *The Poet's Billow*, and *Streetlight Magazine*. She received the Mary Jean Irion Prize from Chautauqua Literary Arts Friends in 2015 and was a finalist for the 2015 Bermuda Triangle Prize (*The Poet's Billow*) and the 2019 Patricia Dobler Poetry Award. A professor emeritus at University of Virginia's School of Education, she earned a Master of Fine Arts from Vermont College of Fine Arts in 2015.

Brendan Stephens teaches creative writing at East Carolina University. He received his PhD in creative writing and literature at the University of Houston. His work has appeared in *Epoch*, *Southeast Review*, *Notre Dame Review*, *Carolina Quarterly*, and *SmokeLong Quarterly*.

Chelsea Stickle is the author of the flash fiction chapbook *Breaking Points* (Black Lawrence Press, 2021). Her stories appear in *Cheap Pop*, *Craft*, and *McSweeney's Internet Tendency*. Her micros have been selected for *Best Microfiction 2021* and the *Wigleaf* Top 50 in 2022. *Everything's Changing*, her second chapbook, was published by Thirty West Publishing this year. She lives in Annapolis, Maryland.

Katerina Stoykova is the author of several award-winning poetry books in English and Bulgarian, as well as the senior editor of Accents Publishing. Her latest book, *Second Skin* (ICU Press, 2018), received the Vanya Konstantinova biannual national poetry award, as well as a grant from the European Commission's program Creative Europe for translation and publication in English. Her poems have been translated into German, Spanish, Ukrainian, Bangla, and Farsi, and a volume of her selected poems, translated into Arabic by acclaimed poet Khairi Hamdan, was published from Dar Al Biruni Press in 2022.

SM Stubbs co-owned a bar in Brooklyn until recently. He is the recipient of a Bread Loaf scholarship and is the winner of the 2019 Rose Warner Poetry Prize from The Freshwater Review. His work has appeared in numerous magazines, including *Poetry Northwest*, *Puerto del Sol*, *Carolina Quarterly*, *New Ohio Review*, *Iron Horse Literary Review*, *Crab Creek Review*, *December*, and *The Rumpus*.

Virgil Suárez's tenth volume of poetry, *The Painted Bunting's Last Molt*, was published by University of Pittsburgh Press in 2020.

Emma J. Sullivan is a writer and artist living in Springfield, Missouri. She is currently earning an MA in English at Missouri State University.

Michaella Thornton earned her MFA in creative nonfiction from the University of Arizona. Her work has appeared in *Brevity, The Citron Review, Complete Sentence, HAD,* and *The Southeast Review,* among others, and has been nominated for the Best of the Net, Pushcart Prize, and Best Microfiction series.

Katie Tian is a sixteen-year-old Chinese-American writer and journalist from New York. Her work is published or forthcoming in *Frontier Poetry, Polyphony Lit, The Rising Phoenix Review,* and *Kissing Dynamite,* among other journals. She has been recognized for her writing by Hollins University, Smith College, the Adelphi Quill Awards, and the Alliance for Young Artists & Writers.

Meg Tuite is the author of five story collections and five chapbooks, with her latest being *White Van* (Unlikely Books, 2022). She won the Twin Antlers Collaborative Poetry award for her poetry collection, *Bare Bulbs Swinging,* and is included in *Best of Small Press 2021.* She teaches writing retreats and online classes hosted by Bending Genres and is also the fiction editor of *Bending Genres* and associate editor at *Narrative Magazine.*

Sean Turlington is a recent graduate of Missouri State University's MA in English program and is transitioning into teaching composition while continuing to work on his own writing.

Cameron Vanderwerf is an MFA student in the creative writing program at Hollins University.

J. Haase Vetter is a teacher and writer living with her partner and children in the Pacific Northwest.

Sara Moore Wagner is the winner of the 2021 *Cider Press Review* Editors Prize for her book *Swan Wife* (2022) and the 2020 *Driftwood Press* Manuscript Prize for Hillbilly Madonna (2022). She is also 2021 National Poetry Series Finalist and the recipient of a 2019 Sustainable Arts Foundation award. Her poetry has appeared in many journals and anthologies, including *Sixth Finch, Waxwing, Nimrod, Beloit Poetry Journal,* and *The Cincinnati Review,* among others.

Kieron Walquist is a queer, neurodivergent writer from Missouri. His work appears or is forthcoming in *Bennington Review*, *Gulf Coast*, *Iron Horse Literary Review*, *The Missouri Review*, and other journals. He holds an MFA in poetry from Washington University in St. Louis.

Mike White's second collection, *Addendum to a Miracle* (Waywiser, 2017), was awarded the Anthony Hecht Poetry Prize, judged by Gjertrud Schnackenberg. Individual poems have appeared in *The New Republic*, *Poetry*, *Ploughshares*, *The Iowa Review*, *Kenyon Review*, *The Threepenny Review*, and *The Yale Review*. He lives in Salt Lake City and teaches at the University of Utah.

Ian C. Williams is a poet and educator whose debut collection of poems, *Every Wreckage*, is forthcoming from Fernwood Press in 2023. He earned an MFA from Oklahoma State University, and his poems have appeared in *Crab Orchard Review*, *Harpur Palate*, *The Minnesota Review*, and *Salamander*, among others. His chapbook, *House of Bones*, is available from the National Federation of State Poetry Societies. He lives in Stillwater, Oklahoma.

Lauren D. Woods is a Washington, DC, writer. Her work has appeared in *The Normal School*, *The Antioch Review*, *The Forge*, *Fiction Southeast*, *Literary Hub*, *Wasafiri*, *Hobart*, and elsewhere.

Ellen June Wright was born in England and currently lives in northern New Jersey. She is a retired English teacher who consulted on guides for three PBS poetry series. Her work was selected as *The Missouri Review's* Poem of the Week in June 2021, and she is a Cave Canem and Hurston/Wright Foundation alumna and received five 2021 Pushcart Prize nominations.

Daniel Zeiders is a graduate of Oklahoma State University and lives in Texas.

Winnie Zeng is from Zhejiang, China. She received her MFA from the University of Washington and currently teaches English in her hometown. Her poetry and translations have appeared in *Poetry Northwest*, *Black Warrior Review*, and *Hayden's Ferry Review*, among other journals.

The Orbit of Meter

Writings on Poems and Prosody by Robert Wallace

Edited by James S. Baumlin and Anne Marie Baker
Foreword by Christine Wallace

Coming in May 2023 From the Ozarks Studies Institute
ozarksstudies.missouristate.edu

MAR

Join us as we return to our regular editorial
and connections calendar.

---

subscribe: www.bgsu.edu/midamericanreview
One-year subscription (two issues): $15
Current issue: $9 Back issues: $5

submit: marsubmissions.bgsu.edu

connect: casit.bgsu.edu/marblog

 @MidAm_Review midamericanreview

 Mid-American Review midamericanreview

Department of English • Bowling Green State University
Bowling Green OH 43403
mar@bgsu.edu • 419-372-2725

Don't miss a single word.

Printed in the USA
CPSIA information can be obtained
at www.ICGtesting.com
JSHW020714111023
49721JS00005B/24